547 Easy Ways to

SAVE ENERGY

in Your Home

Roger Albright

Illustrations by Penny Lee

GARDEN WAY PUBLISHING
CHARLOTTE, VERMONT 05445

Illustrations by Penny Lee

Printed in the United States
Third printing November, 1980

Library of Congress Cataloging in Publication Data

Albright, Roger, 1922–
   547 easy ways to save energy in your home.

   Bibliography: p.
   Includes index
   1. Dwellings—Energy conservation. I. Title.
TJ163.5.D86A43   696   78-964
ISBN 0-88266-127-2
      0-88266-126-4 (pbk)

Contents

Introduction

This book isn't intended to be the authoritative, expert, last word on anything. It isn't intended to be encyclopedic on any subject. It isn't intended to transform the world, or build a new society.

It is intended to be a relatively easygoing guide to saving money by saving energy in and around your home.

It is intended to outline many things you can do yourself for little or no expense to make your budget stop screaming.

Beyond what is surveyed in this book there are many other steps you can take, but they may be either accompanied by large outlays of cash, or require the ministrations of platoons of experts at umpteen dollars an hour each. You don't need to buy a book for assistance with those things. The Yellow Pages are full of fine folks who will help you spend your money, if that's what it takes to make you happy.

There have been many sources for the information herein. Some of it comes from the Apprentice Manual of the Busted Thumbs Union, which is to say, it was acquired with hammer in hand. More advanced, some of it comes from the Journeyman's Handbook in that same Craftsman's League, which is to say you are being given the benefit of my mistakes.

Then there are government documents, miscellaneous books, equally miscellaneous friends, and the staff of the publishing company. Each of these sources had a hand in this compilation, or contributed nuggets of information.

I would suggest that you make a checklist as you leaf through these pages. The list can be a roster of the things you plan to do, with a note of the page number where there is information to help. Then you will enjoy a certain sense of nobility and accomplishment as you cross out the items on your checklist one by one.

If you can possibly arrange it, try not to tackle any of these ideas alone. Without going into lengthy explanations, I can assure you that almost every project suggested here will be completed three times as fast and with many times the pleasure when you do it with someone else. It will be as a cooperative venture in the household that the full fruit of this undertaking will be enjoyed.

Working with illustrator Penny Lee has been a pleasure. Much of the spirit in these pages has bubbled up from her effervescence. If, in addition to information, there is fun for you here, please smile in her direction.

Here's a suggestion. Leave this book lying around where other members of the household might pick it up and read a page or two. That's sure to help in the whole effort. Let it be handy where friends and neighbors can see it, too. But don't lend it. Tell them where they can buy their own copies. That will help our whole effort.

Roger Albright

1

Getting Ready for Winter

So you're standing out in front of the house taking a good look at it. Nice house. Some warm memories inside. Pleasant place. Like it.

Just looking at it that way you couldn't tell, but maybe in addition to being a haven from the troubles of the world, it leaks like a busted balloon.

If that's the case, your home is the enemy of your budget, the destroyer of your plans to save for a vacation, and a secret ally of your predatory fuel supplier. Action is called for.

What you'll be striving for in your residential castle is a place that is secure against invaders. Today, though, the invaders threatening to steal your fortune are sneaky drafts, whistling winds, and the silent cold that comes in the dark of the night.

Your defenses are some tools and a few skills to tighten up the place against the invaders.

If you have some problems, you are aware of them when you are indoors, but the place to begin action to solve them is outdoors. There are various ways to deal with chilly drafts after they get in the house, but the better way is to stop them at the threshold, so to speak, before they get inside.

The effect you're reaching for is an airtight package. You won't get that result, and if you did the air indoors would eventually get too stale to breathe. Don't worry about that. Except in a handful of homes being built today with that very idea in mind—an airtight capsule—the average place will continue to "breathe," and there will be plenty of fresh air, even after you do your best to fill the cracks.

And filling the cracks is essentially what you're up to. Here's why. A crack just 1/8th of an inch wide around an average door is just the same as a hole in your wall about four by six inches, or something like a missing window pane.

If you don't already have them, you'll need a few tools for your security effort, but none of them are big, expensive items, and all of them are easy to use. As much time as you have available is what you need. You may not get the whole job done right away, but you can know that every part of your effort pays off in lower fuel bills and more comfortable living.

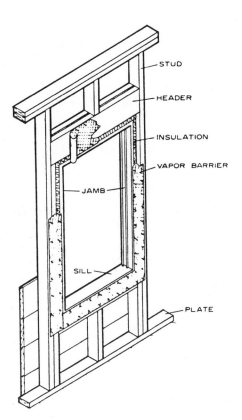

STUD

HEADER

INSULATION

VAPOR BARRIER

JAMB

SILL

PLATE

INSULATING AROUND WINDOWS

A common place to find uninsulated is around window and door frames. Small sections of insulation may be tucked in, but not packed so tightly that the insulating value is lost. Then a vapor barrier should be added.

The best time to get at it is late summer. There's a morning nip in the air to give you an incentive, but it's still warm enough for easy working outdoors. Later on, when winter really hits, some of the things you'd like to do are difficult or impossible, because the caulking and glazing compounds get balky in the cold, and patching cement won't set properly if the temperature is below freezing.

As you read this, is it already too late? Not necessarily. If it's the middle of December there are things you can do on the outside, as well as good resolutions you can make about next year.

Here we go.

Can Cold Air Get in Doors?

A good place to start the security check is with the outside doors. They're in use many times a day all year-round, and are likely to lose their tightness of fit more rapidly than windows. Even if you have storm doors, the main doors need to be checked.

If you can see daylight around the door when it's closed, you have a major job on your hands. You may need to reset the hinges to get a better fit. Adding lathe strips on the inside of the door frame, though, may do the job of covering those gaps, and then you can add weatherstripping to complete the job.

The full weatherstripping job on an outside door should cost about $6, and with a little annual adjusting should last about five years. You'll save about $6 a year in fuel costs, which means the job is paid for in the first year and clear profit for four years thereafter. That's a better return than putting your money in the bank.

There are several kinds of weatherstripping available. Some are better than others. The plastic-and-foam-rubber strips, and the felt strips, are inexpensive and easy to install, but they may not last even one season. You'll be most secure against drafts with a long-lasting

TOO DRY?

Is your home too dry in the winter? Here are two signs of a house lacking moisture.

1. Wooden furniture comes apart.
2. Those in the house complain of dry noses, and often have head colds.

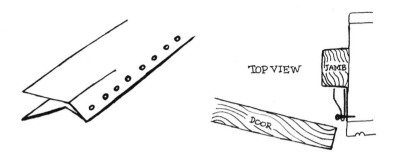

job when you install the spring-metal stripping in your door.

The bottom of the door is the most important place to get a good seal, and the most difficult. If your sill or threshold is quite worn, a tight weatherstrip job is just about impossible, and a new sill is called for. A soft wood such as pine planking is easiest to work with, but won't last a year in a heavy traffic spot. Make it a hard wood like oak, or get a metal doorsill.

To make a weathertight seal, several different products are available. Some go on the sill; some go on the door. The ones that install on the sill are bound to wear out early. They're much easier to install, but they won't last very long.

Installing a weatherseal on the door itself means removing the door (take the pins out of the hinges and it's easy), and probably trimming enough off the bottom to accept the sealing strip. That trimming is tricky, because you must have a straight line. The easiest way to do that is with a circular saw, rather than a plane or a draw-knife. When you've made your cut, put the door back up and make a visual check along the bottom line to be sure your spacing is right, then take it down again and install the weatherstrip.

Almost as important as the door itself is the line where the door-frame meets the house. The door is probably slammed shut more than 1,000 times a year, and that can loosen the caulking around the frame. You can buy a caulking gun and some tubes of caulking compound at

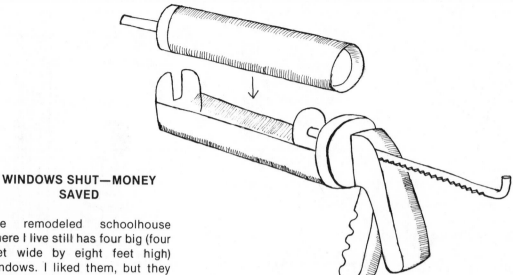

WINDOWS SHUT—MONEY SAVED

The remodeled schoolhouse where I live still has four big (four feet wide by eight feet high) windows. I liked them, but they were an expense every winter. A year or two after I moved in I realized that there was plenty of summer ventilation from other sources, and the big windows were never opened. Now they are nailed shut, their cracks are caulked, and we save a little money in the winter.

any hardware store. Do it. In addition to the bead of caulk around the door-frame, you'll be using the gun in a lot of other places, so it's a good investment.

You have a storm door? Good! Be sure the framing of the storm door is screwed tightly to the door frame.

If you're installing a storm door, put down a bead of caulk across the top and down both sides before you install the frame. Then with the frame screwed in place, you're sure to have a tight and permanent seal against the breezes.

Do a good job on the front door, storm door and all, and you'll save $25 a year or more on your fuel bills, which makes it well worth the effort.

Windows May Waste Heat

Let's check the windows. That may sound like a big chore, if you have a lot of windows in your house. Here's a priority system: the west-facing windows are most likely to catch the prevailing winds, so do them first; the north-facing windows will be exposed to the coldest air, so do them second. The south-facing windows are probably the least vulnerable, so they can wait till last.

• Can you hear your windows rattle in a heavy windstorm? Yes? Then you have an important weatherstripping job to do. Did little breezes sometimes move the curtains even when the windows were closed last winter? Yes? Then you have both weatherstripping and caulking to complete.

• Do you have some windows that are just for looking, but that you never open? Consider shutting them with a permanent seal. Close them securely, then caulk around all four sides. Add a single-pane (cheaper) storm window and bed in a bead of caulk when you install. The end result will be like the double-pane fixed window you may call a picture window in your living room.

• Cracked panes in your windows, or missing putty around the glass, will let cold air leak through. Get replacement panes for cracked or broken panes and tighten up.

• Don't use putty. Use plastic glazing compound. It's different. Putty dries out, cracks, and falls away. That's why you have the repair to make. A good glazing compound will last uncracked for at least ten years, and costs little more than ordinary putty. It's worth the difference.

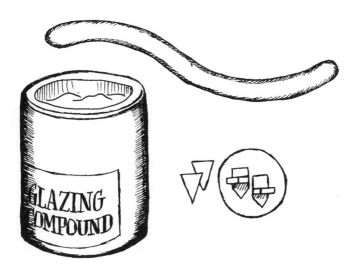

A BUM CHORE

Replacing a broken window in the winter is a bum chore, because the glazing compound gets stiff and intractable. If I have that chore ahead of me I tackle it with two cans of glazing compound: one in hand, and one keeping warmer indoors on the windowsill. By trading them back and forth, the job is possible. If you have only one can of glazing compound, tuck it under your jacket next to your warm body to keep it workable.

Take a glob of glazing compound and roll it between your hands until it has the form of a piece of rope, or a snake. Then line it into the wedge made by the glass and the window frame. This makes a better seal than trying to press the compound in a dab at a time.

• When installing a window pane, there are several kinds of glazier's tips you can use to hold the glass in place before you bead in the glazing compound. Particularly if you're up on a shaky ladder, the odds are good on your breaking the pane with your hammer when putting in some kinds of glazier's tips. Look for the kind with a nib sticking out. You can catch that nib with a screwdriver, tap the screwdriver handle with your hammer, and improve your odds considerably.

• Getting the glass replaced and re-set is the right first step. That completed, a window that is rattling in its frame needs weatherstripping. The most satisfactory method is to install thin spring metal in the channel where the window goes up and down, on the bottom of the window, and on the inside of the bottom rail of the top window, to seal the joint where the two windows meet. This spring metal is available at your hardware store.

• Another possible leakage area is around the window frame. A bead of caulking compound down both sides and at top and bottom should seal out the vagrant breezes, if the window itself is tight.

Storm windows are an excellent buy, particularly in the northern climates. Wooden frames are more efficient than metal frames because they are poorer heat conductors. Single-pane windows are considerably less expensive than double-track and triple-track combination windows. Whatever kind you buy, make sure they fit snugly.

• In aluminum storm windows, the heavier the gauge of the metal and the deeper the tracks, or grooves, that the windows slide in, the better job they will do for you.

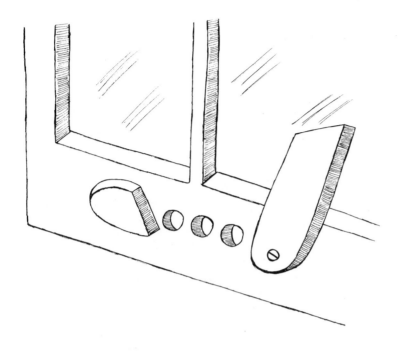

• When installing prefabricated aluminum combination windows, put a bead of caulking compound between the frame of the house window and the new aluminum framing, to be sure there is a full seal to keep out drafts.

• If full storm windows aren't in your budget this year, consider plastic storm covers. Six-mil polyethylene is sold in sheets and rolls at many hardware stores, and it will do a big job.

• With polyethylene sheeting, indoor installation is easier, but not as attractive as installing it on the outside. Indoors, you can put up the sheeting with masking tape, and it will cut back the breezes wonderfully.

• For outdoor installation, measure your plastic to the outer edges of the window frame, cut, and tack through ¼-inch wood slats to hold the plastic firmly to the window frame. A trim, neat job offers minimum opportunity for the wind to catch an edge and tear off the whole thing.

THE OLD STORM WINDOWS

I remember storm windows from my youth; big, cumbersome items that were stored in the attic of the garage, if you bothered to take them down at all. A number was placed on each window frame and windowsill so that they could be matched when it was time to put up the windows. One-inch holes were drilled in the bottom of the frame and covered with a hinged flap that could be opened to let in a little fresh air. All told, a very efficient design. If you still have them, treasure them.

• For a house with smooth wooden siding, measure the plastic to extend beyond the window frame on all four sides and tack through the slats right into the siding. The extra coverage will offer additional protection from seepage around the window frames.

• By installing your plastic storm covers on the outside, you're stopping the cold air before it gets inside, rather than trying to trap it after it enters. Do it carefully, and there will be little distortion in the visibility through the window.

Checking the Foundation

You may have to bend over often to make this final check of the exterior of your home.

Masonry work should be pointed before winter, which means filling the cracks in concrete foundations and facing brickwork. Your hardware store will have ready-mixed mortar for the job, and they'll be glad to sell you a small trowel for applying.

Mix your patching and pointing mortar in an old bucket. Cleaning it out after you're finished will be darned near impossible. If you don't finish your job in one day, hose out whatever mortar remains in it; it won't keep overnight. When the job is finished you can swish the bucket out and hang it in the garage, if you have a place for that kind of storage.

The plank on top of your foundation wall is called a "sill plate." If there is a crack between it and the foundation, put the caulking gun to it and fill that crack. For any crack a half-inch or more wide, fill first with wadded insulation, or with oakum used by plumbers and chandlers, then seal with caulking compound.

If you have a major break in the foundation, patching may not be enough. Make a wooden frame, or form, that will cover the crack at least two inches on each side and at least an inch thick, then pour mortar into the form for a thorough job. Let it set at least twenty-four hours before removing the form.

The lapped siding used in many traditional homes can develop cracks over the years, and they should be sealed with caulking. The best time to do it is just before painting. However, the caulking job doesn't have to make your house look like a patchy mess, because caulk comes in a variety of colors, and you can pick out a fairly close match.

Be sure that your cellar windows are closed tightly through the winter. More cold can enter your home through a small, ground-level window than through the picture window in your living room.

Consider boarding over those cellar windows for the cold season, or at least giving them a double polyethylene covering.

Evergreen shrubbery around the base of your home has much more than a decorative purpose: it cuts the force of the wind at your home's most vulnerable point. Those evergreens are most important on the northern and western sides, where the winds will be strongest.

Been thinking about a tool shed? There are metal structures you can put up in your yard, but you'll get more for your money with a shed built right against the house. There it will serve as dead-air insulation against the wall and also stop the drafts from sneaking through that section of the foundation area.

If you're going to build an attached tool shed, the best location is on a west wall; next best on a north wall, for fuel-saving purposes.

The same logic as applies to a tool shed also follows for a dog house. A separate structure may be cute

HOW YOU USE ENERGY

Pennsylvania State University says this is how energy is used at home:

Heating of space 57.5%
Water heating 14.9%
Refrigeration 6.0%
Cooking 5.5%
Air conditioning 3.7%
Lighting 3.5%
Television 3.0%
Food freezer 1.9%
Clothes drying 1.7%
Others 2.3%

It can be seen that the big energy users in the home are heating of space and water heating, totaling 72.4%. This is where the most can be accomplished in saving energy.

—Snoopy likes his—but one attached to the house has fuel-saving advantages.

If you have an outside tank for fuel oil, consider a framed cover for it. Sheltering it from the elements will minimize evaporation from sun heat, will tend to keep it from getting too cold for the oil to flow in sub-zero temperatures, will add some insulation and draft-cutting factors to your house, and will be more attractive.

About that cover for the oil tank: Most local building codes wisely won't let you make that a conventional air-tight structure. Be sure it is well vented so fumes won't accumulate and explode.

If you have perennial flower beds at the base of your house, you may bank them with straw in the fall to protect the plants. Good idea. While you're at it, take into account that the straw is extra insulation around the base of your house. Let your straw bed be deep and generous, but be sure to remove it in the spring or you'll run the risk of rotting the wood.

The next time you paint your house, or put on a new roof, keep in mind that the darker colors absorb heat from the sun, while those light, bright colors reflect heat away that you might be using to advantage.

Long Johns and a Warm Hat

2

Long Johns
and a Warm Hat

The purpose of insulation can be stated simply: to keep the warmth on one side of the barrier, and the cold on the other. That purpose is accomplished by stopping the movement of air through cracks and crevices in walls and ceilings, and by trapping dead air in walls and ceilings.

The dead air stops the cold outside from getting inside. As you know, a single pane of glass will stop the whistling breezes from coming in, but it won't stop the cold. The glass itself will get cold and drop a fall of coolness into the room. The answer is two panes of glass with dead air trapped in between, or even three panes, and as much as two full inches between panes.

What you're after is to keep the coldest air from getting in your house at the bottom, and stopping the warm air from getting out through the top. In new home construction, full insulation of walls, attic, or roof is easy. In your existing home getting into the walls will be difficult or impossible, but you probably can reach the important places at top and bottom.

It's important to keep the dead air idea in mind. It's like the fishnet long johns that are worn by arctic explorers. They will keep the body warmer than layers of solid clothing. The different kinds of insulation you can buy for your home are mostly air, which is just right. Properly installed, they help to create that dead air barrier you want.

16

Because it is a fairly good thermal conductor, a stone outer wall is poor in insulation value. The same can be said for brick and concrete. Sheet metal, for the so-called tin roof, single-pane glass, stucco, and roofing shingles all fall in the same category: very little insulation value.

Lumber, composition board, and earth walls have some insulation value, but the real winners are the expanded glass and mineral fibers you can buy as fiberglass, rock wool, and vermiculite, which are designed to have substance while being mostly a trap for air.

Crumpled paper and dry straw also can serve that air-trapping purpose, but are a fire hazard and should never be used. Dry paper can catch fire even though it is encased in a tightly sealed box made of steel a quarter-inch thick.

A thorough job of insulation can save as much as 50 percent on the winter fuel bills, so we're talking about the major item in this business of saving energy. The cheerful thing about this undertaking is that every step is prof-

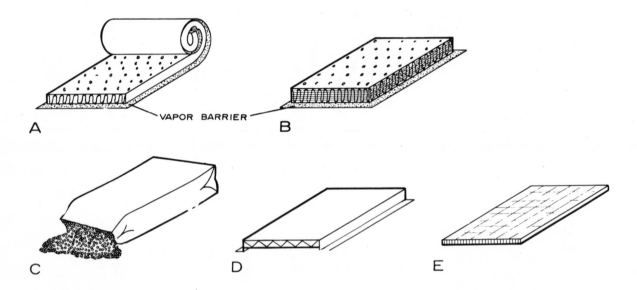

VAPOR BARRIER

A   B

C   D   E

YOUR CHOICE

If you are planning further insulation in your home, you have a choice of materials that can be confusing. Five of them are shown here. *Blanket insulation (A)* comes in 16-inch and 24-inch widths, and in rolls or packages. Common thicknesses are 1½, 2, and 3 inches, and the blanket may be made of mats of mineral or vegetable fibers, such as rock or glass wool, wood fiber, or cotton. If there is a vapor barrier on one side, that side should face the warm side of the wall.

Batt insulation (B) is also made

of fibrous material, in 16-inch and 24-inch widths, and in four- and six-inch thicknesses, and with or without the vapor barrier. *Loose fill insulation (C)* includes rock or glass wool, wood fibers, shredded redwood bark, vermiculite, and wood pulp products, and can be bought in bales or bags. Its common use is between the ceiling joists in unheated attics.

Reflective insulation (D) includes aluminum foil, sheet metal with tin coating, and paper products coated with a reflective oxide composition. The reflective surface, to be effective, must face an air space at least ¾ of an

inch deep. It is widely used in the south to prevent heat flow through ceilings and walls in the summer.

Rigid insulation (E) includes the slab or block insulation that is ½ to 3 inches thick and two by four feet in size. Others are building boards, sheating, and wallboard, which have a structural purpose as well.

Gaining popularity are the expanded polystyrene and urethane plastic foams which are molded or foamed in place. Either may be obtained in board form in thicknesses from ½ to 2 inches.

it. Even if you don't accomplish everything, each insulation factor checked off on your list will be a money-
saver.

When Insulating,
Start at the Bottom

If you're ready to add insulation to your home, start at
the bottom.

You have a cellar that is used only for storage and
utilities. The first insulation step is to put a barrier between the cellar and the rest of the house. In effect, this is
insulating the floor of your first story. Batts or blankets
of rock wool are the easiest bet.

Before you rush out to buy, measure. If the floor joists
are spaced on sixteen-inch or twenty-four-inch centers,
you're in luck, because those are the standard widths for
batts or rolls of insulation. The standard length for batts
is eight feet, so you can figure how many batts you're going to need for the under-floor area you're working with.

Standard insulation rolls and batts have a vapor barrier on one side. You want that vapor barrier to be facing
the warmth, which means in an under-floor installation
the vapor barrier goes up. If you have a problem of fit-
ting, it may be solved by tacking up lengths of wire mesh
or chicken wire and then sliding the insulation on top of
the wire between the floor joists.

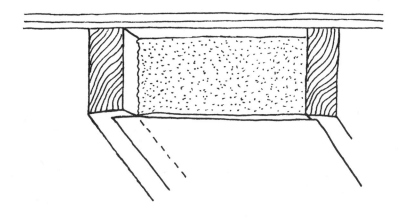

You'll get some added insulation value if you use an inexpensive particle board instead of the wire mesh to hold up the under-floor insulation panels.

Caution. That under-floor insulation, if you do your job right, may leave the cellar really cold. That's OK, unless there are water pipes running through the cold area. The cold water pipes may need to be wrapped to prevent freezing, and the hot water pipes should be wrapped to avoid chilling the water you are paying to heat.

Another caution: If you have a forced warm air furnace in that space you're making colder, consider insulating the heating ducts leading from the furnace. Duct insulation is available in two-inch thickness and is easy to install. Seal the joints between sections of insulation with masking tape.

While you're working on those heating ducts, check the seams between sections to be sure they are tight. If you have any doubts, there is available a metallic tape in several widths that is dandy for sealing those duct junctures before you install insulation. The wider tape is easier to work with.

All you have underneath is a crawl space? Insulation will do a good job there, too. Choose a day when you are feeling calm and even-tempered, and wear old

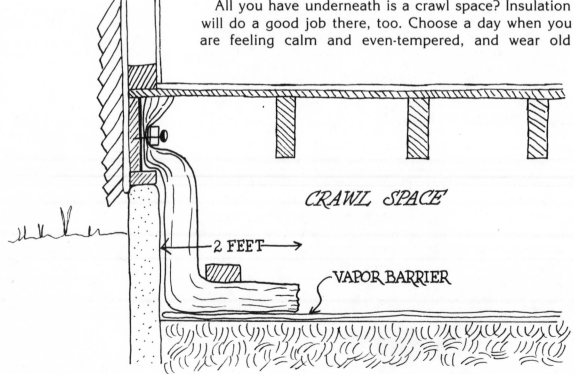

CRAWL SPACE

← 2 FEET →

VAPOR BARRIER

clothes. An under-house crawl space will try your patience, skin your knuckles, and certainly leave you with bumps on your head and cobwebs in your ears.

In handling insulation such as fiberglass, a mask over nose and mouth is a wise idea to avoid breathing those tiny glass particles.

Plan one trip into the crawl space just for measuring. Do a good job and make notes. Then you can cut your materials outside, instead of struggling with that part of the job while you're flat on your back with spiders crawling into your collar and dust sifting into your eyes.

Your materials are six-mil polyethylene for a vapor barrier, R-11 blankets of fiberglass—that's the stuff that's about three inches thick—and strips of scrap wood for nailing. The sketch will give you an idea of how it's done. The board to hold the batts in place can be scrap 2x4's or anything else that's handy, including that rock that's gouging your shoulder blade. All you want is a weight to keep the insulation positioned where you need it.

How did you get into that crawl space? Through a trapdoor, an entry hatch, or a ventilation opening? Be sure any outer entry is closed tightly and insulated, if possible, or some of your effort will have been in vain.

Chances are there are some pipes leading to the kitchen sink going up an outside wall in the crawl space, and maybe some other water pipes as well. Before you leave, be sure they are well wrapped against the cold. They may not have frozen in other years, but now that under-floor area is going to be colder.

The security of those exposed water pipes is doubly important if the pipes are PVC or another of the plastics. The plastic pipes aren't as likely to burst as copper or galvanized, but they are the devil to thaw if they are blocked with ice, because you can't use either blowtorch heat or electric resistance treatment on them.

Providing for summertime ventilation in the crawl space is important to avoid wood rot and mildew problems. Take that into account as you are installing your insulation.

FIGURING THAT INSULATION

We were in between at our house, with an unused, unfinished attic that we planned to finish into three rooms. After the windows were installed, we fully insulated the end walls. Two of the rooms were to be open to the roof-peak, so in them the roof was insulated. The third room had a flat ceiling installed, so insulation was put in the ceiling before the Sheetrock panels went up. For the full length of the attic, sidewalls went up about five feet, and they were insulated before the finish walls were installed.

That left the dead storage space under the eaves to account for. Insulating that floor completed the job.

On the other hand, let's say you have a cellar area that is used for a variety of purposes that require it to be heated, like laundry areas, play areas, and indoor gardening efforts. Then insulating the walls is the task at hand, and it's easy, even if the existing walls are poured concrete or cinder blocks.

On the outside walls, you'll be building another facing wall with 2X3's. The bottom plate will just sit on the concrete floor, not nailed to anything. The top plate can be nailed to the floor joists above it, then the vertical studs should be cut to fit snugly, or slightly force-fit, to be sure the whole works is going to stay in place.

Insulation to fit on twenty-four-inch centers, R-7 in insulation quality (about two inches thick), will do well, so your vertical studs must be positioned accordingly. This

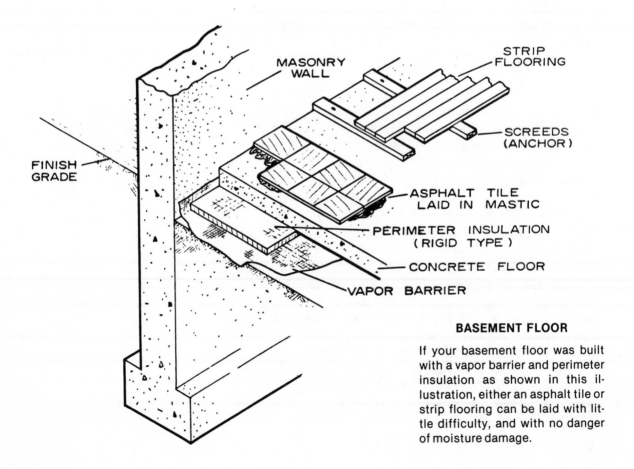

BASEMENT FLOOR

If your basement floor was built with a vapor barrier and perimeter insulation as shown in this illustration, either an asphalt tile or strip flooring can be laid with little difficulty, and with no danger of moisture damage.

WORRIED ABOUT MOISTURE?

If you're unsure of what lies beneath the concrete of your basement floor, and thus are worried about possible moisture problems with a tile or strip flooring, here are the steps to take:

If you want to install strip flooring, place a vapor barrier over the entire floor, and install insulation along the perimeter as shown.

Anchor 2X4's as furring strips spaced twelve to sixteen inches apart across the floor. Nail the strip flooring to these strips.

For wooden tiling, the same vapor barrier, insulation and furring strips are installed, then a 5/8-inch plywood is laid as a base for the tile.

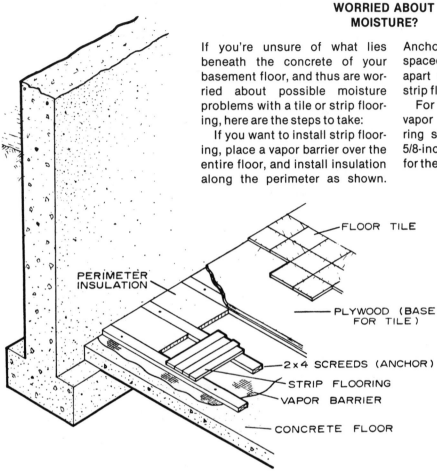

PERIMETER INSULATION

FLOOR TILE

PLYWOOD (BASE FOR TILE)

2 x 4 SCREEDS (ANCHOR)

STRIP FLOORING

VAPOR BARRIER

CONCRETE FLOOR

isn't a bearing wall holding up house weight, so your construction can be simple.

This new wall will give you an opportunity to have electrical outlets where none was practical before. Position them and install the wiring before you place the insulation.

Install the insulation panels from the top down to where the frost line is expected to be. In the northern states, that probably means running the insulation all the way down to the floor. The vapor barrier on the insulation panels should be facing the room. If the batts or rolls you buy don't have a vapor barrier, sheets of six-

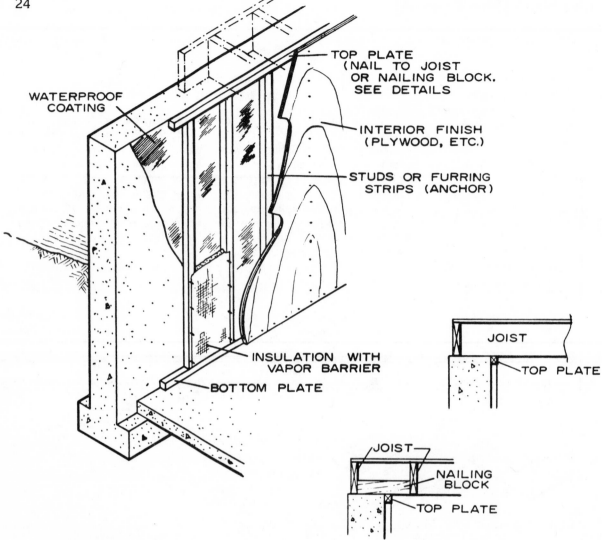

WATERPROOF COATING

TOP PLATE
(NAIL TO JOIST
OR NAILING BLOCK.
SEE DETAILS

INTERIOR FINISH
(PLYWOOD, ETC.)

STUDS OR FURRING
STRIPS (ANCHOR)

INSULATION WITH
VAPOR BARRIER

BOTTOM PLATE

JOIST

TOP PLATE

JOIST

NAILING
BLOCK

TOP PLATE

BASEMENT WALL

Here are the steps recommended by the U.S. Department of Agriculture in finishing a basement wall:

1. Waterproof the wall if there is any possibility of moisture problems. Apply one of the many waterproof coatings to the inner surface of the masonry.
2. Install 2X2's as top plates, anchoring them to the joists, the joist blocks or the wall.
3. Anchor 2X2 bottom plates to the floor at the junction of the wall and floor.
4. Use 2X2's or larger as studs or furring strips.
5. Install electrical outlets and conduit.
6. Place insulation with vapor barrier between the furring strips.
7. Install interior finish of plywood, gypsum board, or other material.

mil polyethylene should be installed over the insulation after it is put in place.

Cover the insulated wall with whatever suits your fancy, taking into account the fact that cellars can be damp. Sheetrock or gypsum board can be quickly ruined if there is water on the floor. So can plywood, unless it is exterior construction grade, which is expensive. Plain pine wood paneling is a good bet.

If floor water may be a problem, you can run almost any kind of wallboard down to about six inches from the floor, then cover the gap with a board molding of eight-inch planks. Don't run the wallboard down to the floor, or it will act like a wick and draw water up to ruin your wall.

Above your new wall, between the floor joists and at both ends, will be exposed areas where insulation is needed. Place it vertically to meet the floor above and also across the top of your new wall. This won't be the most beautiful thing that's happened to your house, but it is practical, and you won't see it at all when you finally get around to putting in a ceiling.

Saving Money in the Attic

The attic is one of the best places for saving money, if your insulation is skimpy or non-existent.

Let's say your attic is completely unusable space

under a truss roof, and isn't insulated. You have two alternatives: blankets of fiberglass or rock wool, or bags of loose fill. If the space is going to be easy to get at, and the spacing of the rafters is a standard sixteen or twenty-four inches, choose fiberglass or rock wool batts or rolls. If, on the other hand, what's up is a crawling job with a lot of irregular spaces, choose the bags of loose material.

Among the bags of material, vermiculite and perlite have about the same insulating value as other materials, are significantly more expensive, but have the advantage of sneaking into smaller crevices. Cellulose fiber has about 30 percent more insulation value than rock wool for the same poured thickness.

If you choose batts or blankets, plan to have about ten inches of thickness in insulation on that attic floor. If you use the bags of loose fill, plan on about eight inches thickness in cellulose fiber, ten inches in rock wool, or thirteen inches in glass fiber.

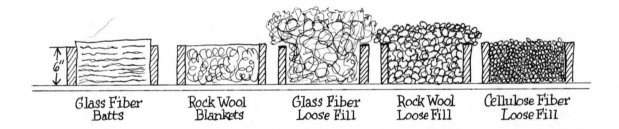

| Glass Fiber Batts | Rock Wool Blankets | Glass Fiber Loose Fill | Rock Wool Loose Fill | Cellulose Fiber Loose Fill |

Be sure to place insulation out far enough to cover the top of the outer wall. At the same time, be sure you don't block the vents under the eaves, if there are any. That may mean putting a piece of scrap wood or cardboard at each end of each run with the loose fill to avoid plugging necessary ventilation.

With the batts, the vapor barrier goes down. With loose fill, put down strips of six-mil polyethylene before installing the insulation, unless the spaces are so irregular or inaccessible that such a vapor barrier placement is impossible.

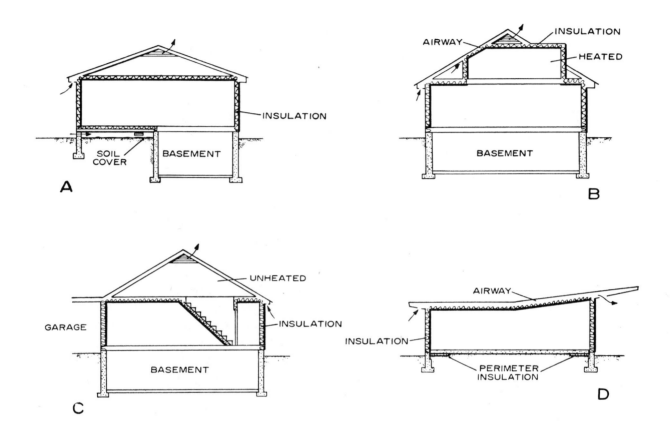

You'll be running into light fixtures and a maze of wires up there, in all likelihood. Insulation should never be in contact with bare wires. BARE WIRES! Call the electrician!

The loose fill is fire-resistant and can be in contact with the boxes that hold electrical connections. With batts and blankets, be sure that any paper coverings are peeled back or cut off to at least three inches away from any electrical junctions or fixtures.

Let's say now that you have an unfinished attic, but the floor is already in place. If you're not going to use the attic, and there's no reason at all to heat it, now or in the future, your best bet will be to tear up the floor and put insulation between the exposed floor joists. Then you can put the floor back down again so the attic can be used as unheated storage space.

WHERE TO INSULATE?

These illustrations from the U.S. Department of Agriculture's *Wood-Frame House Construction* show where insulation should be placed under a variety of situations.

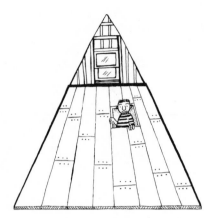

Alternatively, let's suppose the attic space is going to be used as a sewing room, play room, workshop, or other purpose that requires heating. Then you'll want to insulate the roof.

Chances are your roof beams are on twenty-four-inch centers, so there will be standard batts in the six-inch fiberglass or rock wool insulation that will fit for insulating the roof. If yours is an older house you may not have those standard spacings, in which case you'll have to cut batts to fit, or buy sheets of polyurethane board and cut to fit.

If you use the plastic panels, the way to buy is by "R" numbers. Without explaining what that's all about, you'll be looking for "R-30." The panels come in thicknesses of ¾ inch to 4 inches, with R ratings to match, and they differ with the different kinds and brands.

Caution: The plastic panels made of polystyrene and urethane have high insulation value for their thickness, and they are their own vapor barrier. Glass fiber board requires a separate vapor barrier. The caution is that the plastic panels exude deadly fumes if there is a fire in your home, and they should be covered with gypsum board (Sheetrock) panels to minimize that danger.

Some added notes on attics:

When you're working up there, be sure you have boards to walk on and an extension light to help you see what you're doing. When walking on the floor joists, it only takes one slip to send you to the hospital, because that ceiling under you won't support you, and you'll fall right through.

Overhead, be careful at all times to steer clear of the roofing nails that are sticking through, or you'll get that hole in your head you've been hearing about all these years.

The end walls can also be hazardous, because the nails that secured the outer siding are almost certainly sticking through. If your house has any years on it at all, those roofing and siding nails are dirty and rusty, and good candidates to give you a serious infection. If you get a

SLIGHTLY IRREGULAR

My house was built in the 1880s, before many measurements were standardized. The spacing of floor joists, wall studs, and ceiling rafters is what might be called random. At least I can discover no plan in it, although it might have to do with the spacing of the original windows. Insulating is a headache when that's the situation, but it can be done. You just cut and measure each piece crossways and fit it in.

puncture wound up there in the attic, don't mess around with it. Get to a doctor right away.

Before you begin insulating, check the exposed roof areas for stains and discolorations on the wood. They indicate leaks. They may not be apparent downstairs, but you'll have a mess on your hands if you don't patch those holes. Wet insulation is ineffective and may damage your home by holding moisture and causing rot.

Chances are the attic rooms you want to use will heat themselves in the winter with what naturally rises from the house beneath, unless the attic floor is well insulated. Running heating ducts to the attic is probably unnecessary.

If you expand your living space by making use of attic rooms, avoid running water pipes up there if you can. If there are no water pipes, the rooms can be closed off when not in use with no danger of pipes freezing and breaking.

If you have an unheated attic with a floor down for storage ease, then there's a place for that worn carpeting when you re-do the living room. Put it down on the attic floor. It may not look wonderful, but who cares? It will add a measure of insulation, and you may be the first on your block with the luxury of wall-to-wall carpeting in the attic.

Check the door to your unheated attic, and to any other unheated area in the house. That door should be treated like a door to the outdoors: closed whenever possible, and weatherstripped if needed.

GETTING IT EVEN

A common problem encountered with fill insulation is getting the desired thickness of insulation between the ceiling joists. A leveling board, as shown in this illustration, can be built quickly, then pulled along between the joists to level the insulation. Note the vapor barrier placed under the insulation.

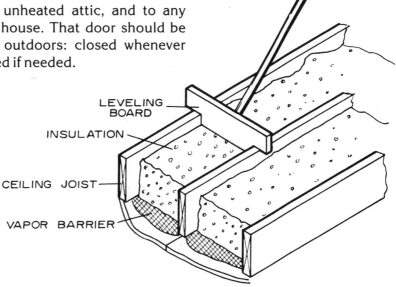

LEVELING BOARD

INSULATION

CEILING JOIST

VAPOR BARRIER

When you plan to open extra rooms in the attic, be sure to include the cost of double or triple pane windows in your estimates, or the project may wind up costing you a lot more than you imagined. The heat loss through attic windows can be more than twice the loss through those downstairs.

About home insulation in general:

If yours is an older home that has never been insulated, consider selling it or tearing it down. Getting insulation into old walls is an expensive and uncertain procedure. There's no easy way you can tackle it yourself, and the commercial applicators who use machinery to blow insulation into walls are faced with many problems that complicate their work.

But you love the old place. Well, room by room you can remove the indoors side of the outer walls and start insulating. Your first layer will probably be wallpaper, then plaster, then wooden lath strips, then paper, then—I hate to tell you. Inside the walls will be the dust of the centuries, augmented by whatever the mice have left behind. Have handy a shovel, broom, and vacuum cleaner.

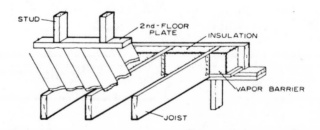

REMEMBER THESE SPACES

In one and one-half and two story homes and in basements, the area at the joist header, as shown in this illustration, should be insulated and protected with a vapor barrier. The barrier is on the warm side of the wall. Vapor barrier materials include aluminum foil and plastic films.

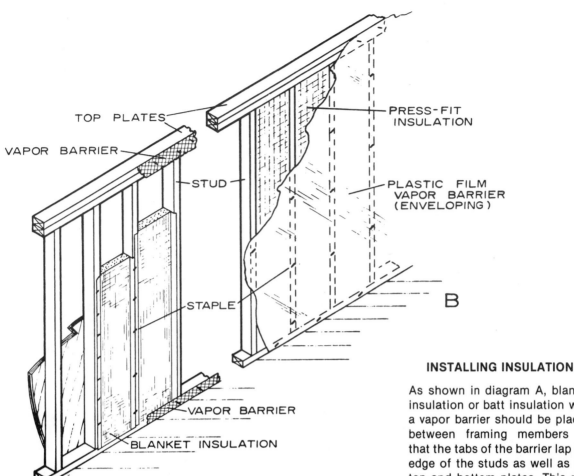

TOP PLATES

VAPOR BARRIER

STUD

STAPLE

VAPOR BARRIER

BLANKET INSULATION

A

PRESS-FIT INSULATION

PLASTIC FILM VAPOR BARRIER (ENVELOPING)

B

INSTALLING INSULATION

As shown in diagram A, blanket insulation or batt insulation with a vapor barrier should be placed between framing members so that the tabs of the barrier lap the edge of the studs as well as the top and bottom plates. This provides a better use of the insulation, although most contractors prefer stapling the tabs to the sides of the studs, since this makes it easier to apply the dry wall or rock lath. Note the narrow strips of vapor barrier applied to the head and sole plates.

In illustration B, press-fit or friction type insulation is fitted between the studs, then a plastic film vapor barrier such as four-mil polyethylene is used to cover the entire exposed wall, including the window and door heads, providing excellent resistance to vapor movement. Using this method, workers cover both door and window openings, then cut away the unwanted film after the wall is completed.

When you get in the wall you'll probably discover that the vertical studs aren't spaced evenly, so standard insulation won't fit. You may also find braces between the studs. Those are firebreaks. They tend to slow down a fire that might otherwise run up through the walls unchecked. They are also the reason why blowing in insulation can be such an uncertain process.

When the outer wall is exposed, fit in the insulation as best you can, first filling in all the cracks around doors and windows. The vapor barrier should be on the warm side of the wall. If there isn't a vapor barrier on the insulation you are using, then a sheet cover of six-mil polyethylene is indicated.

ANOTHER ANSWER

After the insulation has been installed in those old walls in our home, we discovered that putting up Sheetrock on the oddly-spaced studs is too much for the patience and good will of normal people. We didn't try after a lot of measuring showed us that we would go crazy doing it and still not stand a chance of getting decent seams between the panels. Our compromise: a full sheeting of black builder paper, covered by weathered boards from a sugar house we were permitted to tear down. We like it.

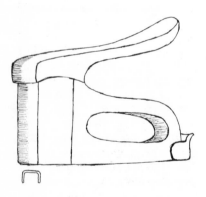

If yours is a newer home and not insulated—although that's not too likely—the process of re-doing the walls isn't going to be too difficult. You may even be able to salvage the panels of Sheetrock if you are very careful when taking them down.

If you have an uninsulated home, new or old, by all means get competitive bids from the commercial firms that blow in insulation, for those parts of the job you don't want to tackle. Spell out in writing just what the applicator guarantees to do, and for what price.

After you have those competitive bids, get one more. The last one should be from an installer of insulated siding who will put a new outer wall around your house. You may discover you can get that big job done with complete wall insulation for something like the price of blown-in insulation plus a paint job. Worth thinking about.

A final thought.

When there is any amount of insulation material to install, there is one super-tool you'll do well to buy. It's the staple gun. There's really no easy way to install batts or blankets of insulation without a staple gun, especially if you're doing overhead work. It's also just about essential for handling polyethylene sheets. Keep it around the house when the insulating chores are completed. You'll find yourself using it for lots of chores, and indispensable if you get into re-upholstering a favorite chair.

Keeping Comfy

3
Keeping Comfy
Room by Room

Some of the advice and counsel available today on fuel economy can be boiled down to this: "How miserable can you stand to be?" Well, that's one approach. It starts off with the injunction to turn your thermostat down to 60° F. and smile nobly as you shiver.

Don't tell the federal energy mogul, but I'm not going to turn my thermostat down to 60. I want to be comfortable. I'm doing my trimming in other ways, which is what this chapter is all about.

There are some rooms where the thermostat can very well be turned down to 60 or less, but not the room where you plan to relax in the evening. There are some places in your house, in fact, where you don't need to have any heat at all, and where the lack of heat is no sacrifice.

Different rooms have different uses in the average home, and what would be too warm for one activity isn't warm enough for another. The ideal answer is a heating system that can be fine-tuned, sending different amounts of heat to different places.

The easiest method for zone heat control is electric heat, where there is no central heating system. Each room has a separate thermostat, making it possible to shut off unused rooms, have cool settings in some rooms and warmer settings in others. You may already know, though, that electric heat is the most expensive and energy-wasteful method for achieving wintertime comfort.

The old-fashioned custom among the wealthy — a little fireplace in each bedroom — was an early variation on the zone-heating theme. One of the servants would go upstairs and light each fire a half-hour before bedtime to take off the chill. Later, as the fire died down and the room cooled, the occupant was asleep and wasn't made uncomfortable. Getting up in the morning could be a chiller unless the servant crew was instructed to kindle new fires before the folks woke up.

Today, the next-best kind of system is a forced warm-air furnace with separate ducts for each room in the house. Each duct can have a butterfly damper to control the flow of warm air to various places in the house, or even to shut off the heat in unused rooms. That isn't as convenient as a system with individual thermostats, because to change the plan means tinkering with the dampers to rebalance the air-flow pattern, which can be a nuisance.

A hot-water heating system with radiators in each room is fairly easy to control with the valves on the radiators, but if you plan to shut off a room, you need to be careful about a radiator full of water in a room where the temperature might go below freezing. A busted radiator is a terrible mess.

One of the more efficient methods is the true central heating system with just one heat source — a furnace or a big stove. It radiates heat through the rooms on the first floor, and warms the upper rooms as the heat rises. Floor registers that can be opened and closed give substantial adjustability, and a room can be closed off just by closing the door and shutting the gravity-flow registers. Few homes today, though, are equipped this way.

So, you make do with what you have, thinking all the time about what the next steps may be — which is the subject of another chapter.

Thermostat: The Key to Savings

Thermostats, where they are in your home, and how you set them, can be instrumental in deciding the size of your winter's fuel bill.

Separate thermostats in bedrooms will save on winter bills. You can, in fact, go as low as 60° F., and still find ways to keep warm in bed, even without an electric blanket.

• When you'll be out for an evening, turn down the thermostats. If you'll be away for a weekend or more, lower the thermostats to 45° F., or to the lowest temperature setting before "off." You'll save on heating without chancing a freezeup of your water pipes.

• When you can shut your house for a few days or more, you'll save a little on the operation of the refrigerator and

SAVE ON FUEL— GO TO BED

About that business of keeping warm in bed. ... We have our television set on a closet shelf, directly in line with the four-poster. When snuggled under a quilt or a down comforter, we keep plenty cozy for evening TV viewing, without heating up our big living room (24 ft. by 28 ft) just for a little time with the boob-tube.

freezer, which won't need to work so hard to maintain their cool.

• How low can your home thermostats be set? We've gotten accustomed to 72° F. as a comfortable norm. Reduce the heat just one degree at a time and try it for a week. Each one-degree drop means about a 3 percent reduction in your fuel bill and — gradually — you might be able to go down three or even four degrees comfortably and save a chunk of money.

• Try turning down the thermostats five to ten degrees at night, and then cranking them up again in the morning when the coffee is heating. If you can get used to that, you'll save five to ten percent of your heating bill.

HOUSEPLANTS HELP

We count on houseplants to provide the extra humidity we need in the winter. The natural respiration of the plants, plus evaporation from the flowerpots, provides enough additional moisture to eliminate the dry-throat problems we had experienced in the past, and to keep the furniture from falling apart. The moist air feels warmer (it isn't the heat, it's the humidity), so less artificial heat is needed, and an electric humidifier is unnecessary.

The cacti and other desert plants are interesting, but by their nature they're not as much help in furnishing humidity when you want it. We have a few, but rely mostly on the broad-leafed natives and different kinds of ivy that demand little attention and give maximum pleasure.

• If you discover that the night thermostat setting is something you can live with, ask an electrician about a two-way thermostat with daytime and nighttime settings that will turn the trick for you automatically.

• Do you need to talk yourself into a lower thermostat setting? Here's an argument. Your plants are healthier in the cooler air.

• The health of your plants isn't in the same discussion with your personal comfort? All right, you'll be healthier in the cooler air. Your body will burn a few more calories keeping you warm, thereby helping you to lose the weight you wanted to lose anyway, to improve your general health.

• When it's time to open the windows for a little fresh air indoors in the spring, remember to turn down the thermostats. Those cool breezes that feel so good will send your furnace on a fuel-burning rampage unless the thermostats are reset.

• Planning a good-sized party? Turn the thermostats down. Each guest is the equivalent of a 175-watt heater, and the gang will warm up the place without the furnace or the heating units in operation.

Economical Lighting

Want to slow down that spinning electric meter? Be careful how you use lights in your home. Here are three ways.

1. Use high-wattage reading lamps for reading. Candles or 25-watt bulbs offer plenty of light for evening conversation, create a pleasant mood for talking, and will reduce electric bills.

THE OLD-FASHIONED LIGHT

Try candlelight or an old fashioned oil lamp at mealtime. There will be less illumination per penny spent, but enough light to enjoy your meal in a warm glow without touching the electric switch.

Kerosene lamps send a lot of heat through their clear glass chimneys. Be sure to keep them away from curtains and other flammables, and for heaven's sake don't touch the chimney until at least a half-hour after the lamp has been put out, or you'll burn your fingers.

When you decide to economize on electricity with the softer glow of kerosene lamps in appropriate places, be sure to find a good place OUTDOORS to store the

kerosene can. Indoors, the kerosene can is a fire hazard, and also a potential drinkable poison for little ones.

2. When you have a choice between incandescent light bulbs and fluorescent tubes, choose the tubes. They use much less power for the same amount of light. You don't like that ghastly blue tone they put out? Check your store for the newer, warm-tone tubes that are much more flattering, and closer to a daylight radiance.

3. Dark walls and ceilings may be dramatic, but they absorb light. Pastels or white on walls and ceilings will give maximum illumination with fewer light fixtures burning in the evening, and will make a room with drapes open pleasantly light without electricity during daylight hours.

LIGHT A CANDLE

I've enjoyed Christmas presents from some of my kinfolk who make candles. Different waxes, colors, and fragrances are available at hobby shops, and you can make them either by the dip or mold method. Some given to me were molded in square milk cartons. They burn for days.

Speaking of Drapes

DRAPERY RODS

Fairly heavy drapes are important in taking advantage of sun heat, and some dime store curtain rods are too flimsy to hold them properly. Decorator drapery rods can get expensive, so I made my own: just plain, round closet rods (available at almost every lumber yard in whatever length you need) held up with brackets scroll-saw cut from wood scraps. Entirely satisfactory. Stain them or paint them to match your room scheme.

By closing drapes and shades at night, you can cut your heat bill by as much as 16 percent. Pull them back during the day, of course, for free light and heat.

In fact, you'll do well to install your drapery rods well over the wall on each side of windows to gain full light and heat benefit by pulling drapes all the way off the windows during daylight.

Because those drapes are important at night when they are pulled to minimize heat loss and cut drafts, we recommend heavy drapery material, or lined drapes.

It is a practical decorator touch to hang old patchwork quilts as window draperies. They'll be heavy enough to do a good job, easy to hang, and will certainly be interesting. Check your local thrift shop.

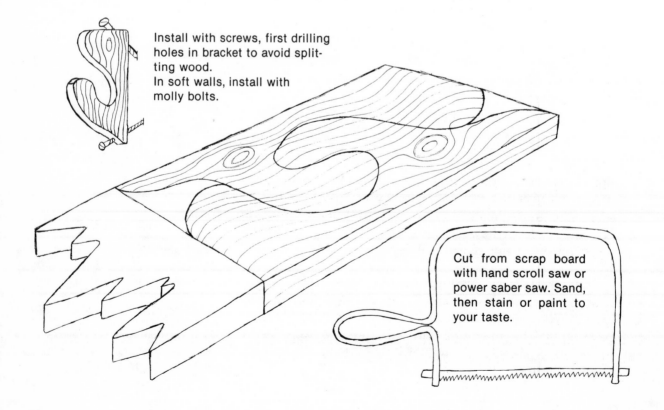

Install with screws, first drilling holes in bracket to avoid splitting wood.
In soft walls, install with molly bolts.

Cut from scrap board with hand scroll saw or power saber saw. Sand, then stain or paint to your taste.

How to Save Heat— And Money

A new door here, new carpeting there, and a change in habits for all members of the family. These things can add up to big energy—and money—savings.

Read through this list, then check off the ones that would save you money.

• Don't leave the room without closing the closet door. There's no need to spend hard-earned money heating storage spaces. For a luxury touch, clothes you're going to wear can be taken out the night before into the room warmth. Be your own valet and save money.

• Ceiling need repainting? Consider soundproof tiles instead. They will not only bring pleasant quietness to the room, but also act as insulation to hold in room heat.

• Instead of just painting or papering walls that are exposed to outside air, think about cork panels, particle board, or wood walls. Over a layer of builder paper ("tarpaper") or plastic sheeting, your new, solid walls will cut drafts, add insulation, and be attractive and easy to care for as well.

• Take those beautiful Oriental throw rugs off the floor and hang them on the walls where people can see and enjoy them, and where they will serve as additional insulation.

• Carpeting on floors even in bathroom and kitchen is a heat-saver and comfort-maker. Durable carpeting is available that is quite practical for these locations. In the bathroom particularly, stepping out of the tub onto a cozy carpet is so much nicer than bracing your toes for those cold tiles. The practical advantage is that the bathroom thermostat can then be set much lower without any discomfort.

**SIX EASY WAYS
TO CUT HEATING COSTS**

Here are six ways to cut your heating costs:

1. For many people, home heating bills can be cut 10 percent or more with one simple move: have the furnace cleaned and adjusted properly. If yours is an oil burner, that means at least an annual inspection by a qualified technician.

2. While your oil burner is under discussion, check and see whether a smaller fuel nozzle can be installed. The burner may operate just as well with a smaller fuel nozzle, and save as much as 15 percent on your fuel bill.

3. Forced warm-air furnaces need to have their air filters cleaned or replaced at least twice each winter. A clogged filter chokes off the necessary breathing of the furnace and makes it work harder.

4. When you're rearranging furniture, be sure that radiators, warm-air registers or heating units aren't blocked from their proper functioning. If there's an arrangement you "must" have that blocks heat flow, let it wait till summer when it won't affect heating efficiency.

5. Many kitchens and bathrooms have exhaust fans to take away unwanted odors, and in some bathrooms they turn on automatically with the light switch. Convenient, but expensive. In winter, those exhaust fans not only take out odors, but they're blowing away warm air as fast as they can. That's expensive. Use them sparingly and save money.

6. A little extra humidity permits a lower thermostat setting without discomfort. Some furnaces will accept a humidifying system easily and inexpensively. If that's not the case with you, try pans of water on radiators or heat registers to put a little moisture in the air.

• Is there a doorway between the first and second floors of your home, or on up into the attic? If not, you should have one. Stairwells act like chimney flues, conducting heat to the top of the house where you need it less. A door may be easy to construct and will tend to keep the heat downstairs where you need it.

• Time for school? Make a habit of getting all the kids out the door at once each day, instead of a separate opening and closing for each one. It'll save enough for extra Christmas presents for all.

• Think about an outdoor doghouse. Remember, your pup's ancestors lived outdoors for centuries, and he can adapt to being outdoors all year-round, unless he happens to be one of the few tropical breeds like a Chihauhau. The wintertime advantage to you is no more opening and closing the door zumteen times a day to let him in and out—and resultant heat loss with each opening. ing.

• Also with the dog outdoors, you may spend less time with the vacuum cleaner humming to pick up dog hairs.

• Take a tip from the department stores: put an extra heating unit or warm air register near the principal entryway. Warming that blast of cold air when the door is opened will keep the main thermostat from turning on so many times, and minimize the drafts that make you so uncomfortable.

• Double doors at the principal entryway make a convenient foyer for winter boots, and also cut heat loss as people go in and out.

• Do you have a game room with a Ping-Pong table? Close it off with a well-fitting door and let it be cooler than the rest of the house. The action of the game will keep the players warm.

• Planning a home workshop? Since the room will not be used regularly, keep it off the main heating system and let it be cool between uses. Warm it with a separate heater or a small wood stove.

• Having the garage within your house framework is convenient in many ways, but be sure to have a separate door for going in and out to the yard or driveway. Every

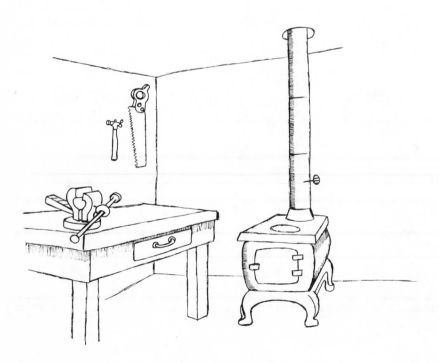

time you open the big garage door is like taking off the side of your house, and costs plenty in lost heat.

• Check around for those relatively useless appliances, and put them on the top shelf of the closet. Singly they don't use a lot of electricity, but together the electric toothbrush, electric shoe-shiner, electric car-washer and the like are items you don't really need. They were invented to sell electricity and sell appliances, not necessarily to help people live better.

• A rug in the children's play area is warmer for playing on the floor than wood or tile. The new indoor-outdoor carpets made of synthetic yarns will take a lot of punishment and are quite stain-resistant.

• I was re-doing a bathroom a few years back and was stuck for a way to locate the warm air outlet. I finally placed it right over the tub/shower. I didn't know it, but that was a happy inspiration. The warm air blowing down is delightful either for tub-bath or shower purposes.

• Go for soft, warm colors in the north rooms where direct sunlight is not available to cheer things up. You'll be surprised at the effect color has on how comfortable you feel.

• Don't forget to close those chimney dampers if you have a fireplace or stove not in use. An open chimney will exhaust more heat than an open window.

CLOSING OFF ROOMS

If you're planning to close off rooms this winter to conserve fuel, don't forget about them. You may have condensation problems.

The U.S. Department of Agriculture makes these recommendations:

1. Do not operate humidifiers or otherwise intentionally increase humidity in unheated parts of the house.

2. Open the windows of unheated rooms during bright sunny days for several hours for ventilation. Ventilation will help draw moisture out of the rooms.

3. Install storm sash on all windows, including those in unheated rooms. This will materially reduce heat loss from both heated and unheated rooms and will minimize the condensation on the inner glass surfaces.

In Summer It's the Heat AND the Humidity

There's lots you can do to keep cool in the summer. You'll be more comfortable this way, and if you have an air conditioner, you'll be saving energy as well.

In the summer, keep an eye peeled for extra lights

burning, particularly incandescent bulbs. They furnish heat as well as light and cause your air conditioner to work harder.

An air conditioner's filter should be cleaned or replaced at least once a month. This reduces the load on the unit, thereby decreasing operating costs.

An air conditioner operates most efficiently when placed on the shady side of your house—normally the north side.

Set your air conditioner thermostat no lower than 78° F., and shut it off if there's a breeze blowing that would cool things off through open windows.

Compare products before you buy an air conditioner. Look for the Energy Efficiency Rating (EER) that you'll find on most appliances today. The higher the number, the more cooling it will produce for a given amount of electricity.

With an air conditioning unit, bigger isn't necessarily better. A unit bigger than you need for the space to be cooled will make the air clammy and uncomfortable; while a unit too small will just work away burning kilowatt hours and still not cool you.

In regard to humidity, in summer you're looking for just the opposite effect from winter: low humidity. The kitchen and laundry areas are moisture-makers, so keep them closed off from the rest of the house as much as possible.

Humidity again: When you take a shower, open the bathroom window to let the moisture out.

More on humidity: In the summer, be sure to cover the pots on the stove when you're cooking to minimize the steam escaping into the room.

The covered pot, incidentally, is a good idea any time. It holds the heat in where it will do the cooking, rather than letting it escape into the room. The covered pot will come to a boil faster, saving fuel when you're making coffee, boiling eggs, or doing any other cooking business that calls for a boil.

Since heat rises, in the summer you'll do well to open upstairs and attic windows to let the heat escape.

Then, in the cool of the evening let the more temperate air into the house and close the windows first thing in the morning to keep that cool air inside.

Awnings can really be a help in the summer. Particularly on the south windows, awnings will keep the sun away while still letting the light and breezes through. A heavy duck cloth, or plastic panels, either one in a light color or white, will be most effective.

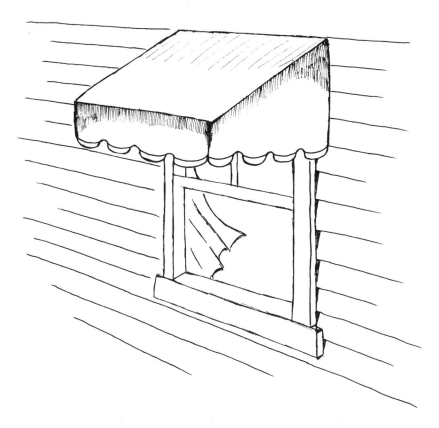

A large window fan costs one-fifth as much as an air conditioner, and uses only one-fourth as much power. Perhaps the most effective place to put it is in an attic window where it will push the hot air out of the house and draw the cooler air in through the downstairs windows.

Bright pastel colors and crisp, cheery plants indoors and out will help to make your home feel cooler.

For cooling breezes in the spring and fall, open windows from the top to exhaust excess heat without making drafts that might trigger the thermostat.

You'll be cooler in a minimum amount of loosely-fitting clothing, but some clothes will help you feel cooler because the moisture evaporating from them as you perspire will feel good on your skin.

Economy in the Kitchen

4

4

Economy in the Kitchen

In many aspects of our living, our daily functioning is made possible by habits we follow. If we had to think about how to brush our teeth, how to tie our shoes, how to put on a jacket—we wouldn't get started in the morning. We can do all those things almost automatically—without thinking—so they get done smoothly and quickly.

Those same habits, though, can be ruinous when the monthly fuel bills arrive because the inexpensive fuels of the past have led us into very wasteful habits, particularly in the kitchen. To achieve important economies doesn't necessarily mean drastic change in the style of living, but it certainly does mean programming yourself with a new set of habit patterns.

Some parts of our lives are optional, but not cooking and eating. What happens in the kitchen is absolutely necessary, and is going to happen every day. That's the reason why a careful examination of how fuel energy is used in the kitchen can be vital to your overall economy plan.

Another truth: Because using the kitchen is an everyday event for all the members of the household—and the kitchen may be the place where much of the shared life takes place—the development of new habits in the kitchen may raise the family consciousness about energy uses in general, and so spill over into other aspects of fuel saving.

Just one example may serve to illustrate. After a meal, we all know it is sensible to put leftover foods in the refrigerator. We all know if they are left out on the kitchen counter overnight, or even for several hours, they'll turn bad and need to be thrown away. There are two ways to use the refrigerator, though.

One way is to take the foods from the table and the pans from the stove and—probably in several trips—stack them in the refrigerator for later use. This way your refrigerator will be gasping for breath and laboring hard to keep its cool, what with hot foods, hot pans and hot dishes to chill, and the door opening and closing several times.

Another way is to put the leftovers in storage containers and let them sit on the counter for a half-hour or so until they cool a little. Then, all in one operation, they can be placed in the refrigerator for storage and later use.

There isn't much difference between those two methods. It's really no more than exchanging an old set of habits for a new set. Considering, though, that the process takes place in your kitchen several hundred times a year, if it saved you no more than a penny a meal (and it will save more than that), you're looking at a saving of almost $11 a year just in the way the refrigerator is used after mealtime. Eleven dollars here, 75 cents there, three dollars the other place; they all add up to making a significant difference, just by changing habits.

There are, of course, other avenues to saving that require investments of time and money. Make no mistake. They're worthwhile. It may be, though, that habit changes in the kitchen and elsewhere will save the most of all with the least effort.

Cool Cash Savings

There's money to be saved in your refrigerator. You may be spending more than you need to just by running your refrigerator at a cooler setting than is required. Put an ordinary household thermometer in the refrigerator for a half-hour or so. If it registers colder than 40° F., change to a warmer setting and check it again.

While you're at it, check the door gaskets all the way around by closing the door on a dollar bill. If the bill slips out easily at any place, you're wasting money. You may be able to correct the problem by putting paper strips or thin cardboard behind the gasket where you spot the leak, or by adjusting the latch. If those don't do it, a new gasket is a good investment and isn't hard to install.

Opening and closing the refrigerator door is what makes extra dividends for the electric power company. Here are some thoughts:

When you stand with the refrigerator door open, thinking about what you'd like to have, you're running up the cost of that snack. Do your best to imagine what's inside before you open the door, and then go directly to it. Try to teach your children this habit, too.

Help yourself and your family by putting a checklist on the refrigerator door, rostering what's inside and also crossing off what's been eaten. That's the snack menu, and it can save many a door opening.

Get organized before meals so that everything needed

SNACK LIST
cheese
cream cheese
apples
oranges
~~lemonade~~ !
coke
sliced ham

can be taken out and placed at the ready on the kitchen counter with just one opening of the refrigerator door. Don't forget the catsup.

After coming home from the store, empty all the shopping bags on the counter, put all the items that need refrigeration in one place, <u>then</u> open the refrigerator door.

After dinner, think about storing the leftovers in the way outlined at the beginning of this chapter, with particular attention to the business of covered containers. This is particularly important with frost-free models, where moisture is drawn from the foods to condense on the refrigerating coils causing the defrost cycle to operate more often. If you don't have covered refrigerator containers, put the leftovers in cereal bowls and cover with a plate.

Convenient plastic containers can be bought in many stores, but you can also save peanut butter jars, cottage cheese containers, and similar packages with lids that can be cleaned to use for storage.

That frost-free feature certainly is a convenience, but a standard refrigerator that must be defrosted by hand a few times a year will use 36 percent less electricity. Also remember when you're buying your next refrigerator that if you really do want the frost-free convenience, look for a model with a power saver switch. It turns off the defrost heater when humidity is low in the winter and may cut operating costs by as much as 16 percent.

While you're refrigerator shopping, ask for the manufacturer's information on average annual operating costs. These may vary by as much as $40 a year.

Having a houseful of teens and their friends can be a lot of fun, but it can also mean overtime chores for the refrigerator. If this is a daily happening consider buying a second-hand refrigerator just for the cold drinks and putting it in the cool of the cellar where it need not work so hard.

If what's up is just an occasional party, the answer may be a washtub full of ice cubes to keep the canned and bottled beverages cool.

When the kids grow up and have nests of their own,

that big refrigerator you once needed may become a liability. A refrigerator operates most efficiently when it's full, and chances are you don't use its capacity. Consider giving one of the kids the big box and buying a smaller model.

When choosing where your refrigerator is placed, keep it away from heat-producers like ovens and dishwashers. An outside wall is a fair idea, particularly if it's a north wall that will tend to be cool both summer and winter.

And try for four inches of air space around the refrigerator, to let the motor heat escape readily. If it's been running hot, you could save as much as $3-$4 a month.

Freezers Can Be Expensive

Most refrigerators today have a freezer compartment. You may also have a separate freezer, or be thinking about one. Here are some freezer economies.

For openers, a freezer will likely be one of your most expensive electrical appliances to operate. A manual-defrost, 14-cubic-foot model will use about 100 kilowatt hours of electricity each month. Multiply your kwh rate (if it isn't on your utility bill, call the power company) by that usage to find your cost. Then consider canning your garden foods instead of freezing.

You'll use 50 percent more electricity with an automatic defrost model. Weigh that against the modest effort of defrosting a couple of times a year.

Consider your separate freezer as if it were a supermarket annex. Plan your meals for several days—even a week—and transfer the freezer foods to the freezer compartment of the refrigerator all in one "shopping trip."

Keep items for which there is frequent call, like ice cream and orange juice, in the freezer compartment so the big freezer won't need to be opened so often.

Transfer big items like hams, roasts, and turkeys from the freezer or frozen food compartment to the

FREEZE THIS SOUP

At our house we make a favorite bean soup with a leftover ham bone and the glaze from the roasting pan. The last step in the cooking is adding fresh celery, onions, and carrots. Just before the last step, we put some of the beans and ham broth in freezer cartons for later use. When it's time for a couple of bowls of soup, the frozen chunk goes right in the pan and the fresh vegetables are added. Delicious, easy, and fuel-saving, particularly if you have time to let the frozen soup thaw before cooking.

refrigerator a day in advance. That way they will thaw gradually and help to cool the refrigerator while they're doing it.

Recommended temperature for frozen foods is 10° F. Put a household thermometer in your freezer and check the temperature. If it's colder than necessary, change the control setting and check again. You may want to run the temperature setting down to zero when you are putting away the harvest from your garden. Don't forget to reset it.

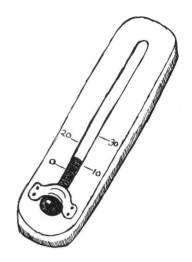

Keep your freezer as full as possible. The bulk of the foods will retain the cold better than empty air, making for more economical operation.

Position your separate freezer in a cool part of the cellar, on the back porch, or out in the garage. These are cooler places, particularly during the winter, and your freezer motor won't need to work so hard. A few trips a week to stock the freezer compartment is a small effort to make for the electricity you'll save.

You'll get extra mileage from your freezer—and your oven—when you cook oversize batches of favorite casseroles and freeze the extra in meal-size packages.

If you have an orderly mind, you can plan to have your separate freezer empty during the growing season when you're eating fresh foods from the garden. Then you can shut it off during the warmest months when it works the hardest.

Putting your frozen foods in well-marked containers, and keeping the frozen supplies in easily recognized categories will make everything easier to find, and therefore mean less time that the door is open while you are searching for something.

A freezer inventory is a good idea. It can be a sheet or small notebook on the wall or on a shelf near the appliance. Menu planning can be done from the inventory, which should include a locator chart so each item can be found easily. Again, less time with the door open.

Baking a pie? Bake three or four and freeze the extras. You'll save money on your oven usage, and those frozen pies will come out weeks or months later ready for a quick warm-up before going to the table.

Leftover waffle batter? Make the waffles, put them in a plastic bag and freeze them. They'll perk up almost like newly made with a few minutes in the toaster, or in your table-top broiler-oven.

A last thought on freezers: The upright models may be somewhat more convenient to use, but every time you open the door the cold "falls out." Chest-type freezers are much more frugal in operation.

TEMPURA PLUS

The first time we made tempura we were carried away with our enthusiasm. We had pieces of fish, shrimps, sliced potatoes, strips of green pepper, sliced mushrooms and onion rings ready to dip in the batter and quick-fry. It turned out to be a lot more than we could eat at one meal. We weren't sure all the ingredients would keep uncooked, so after dinner we cooked the lot, then reheated it for the next day's lunch in the table-top broiler-oven. Yes, it worked out just fine.

Incidentally, we cooked our tempura in a small, cast-iron frying pan. Less heat needed, less oil used; results: excellent.

Cooking the Oriental Way

Cooking is cooking, right? Wrong! Next time you're in town, cruise through the cookbook section at the local bookstore and check on how many different kinds of cooking there are. I'm not about to suggest exotics like lamb's eyeball stew or fricasseed grasshopper, but there are some variations in cooking techniques that can be interesting while they save money at the stove.

In China, cooking fuel has been a scarce and expensive commodity for centuries. To meet the need, the Chinese have developed a method called stir-frying. They do it in a utensil called a wok. You can buy one if you want to be thoroughly authentic, or you can use your frying pan.

Wok and Utensils

The meat and vegetables are cut or sliced into small bite sizes and cooked in a moment in hot oil. A full meal is cooked in minutes. Tasty, economical, and more nutritious, too.

Cooking fuel is precious, too, in overcrowded Japan, where tempura cooking has become one of the answers. Again, it is bite-size pieces in hot oil, but they are dipped in a tasty batter first, quickly fried, and then dunked in one of several appetizing sauces. Another economical treat.

A more conventional way to use the same principle is to cut vegetables into bite-size pieces and cook them in a steamer. They'll cook nearly as fast as with the boiling water treatment, and retain more taste and nutrition in the process.

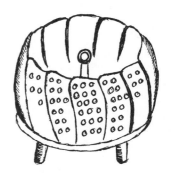

Vegetable Steamer

Try to cut back on the number of burners you fire up to prepare a meal. The ideal here is something like the pot roast where a complete meal is cooked on one burner. There are many variations, including that all-time favorite, corned beef and cabbage with boiled potatoes.

When boiling water, as for soft-boiled eggs or macaroni, turn the burner down as far as you can and still maintain the boil. The water is going to get just so hot and no hotter. Too much heat just makes steam—and wastes money.

When boiling anything on the stove, use the least amount of water possible. The cooking will be done more quickly, you'll waste fewer of the nutrients, and, by keeping the lid on, you will minimize the danger of "running dry."

Don't Forget the Oven

Whether it's gas or electric, the oven in a conventional stove is an energy glutton. The problem is compounded if the oven has a pre-heating feature, and gets even worse if it's the self-cleaning variety. Let's take a look.

One answer to oven efficiency is to get maximum use

WHY BURN A PILOT LIGHT?

If you're buying a new gas range, look for one with electric ignition rather than a pilot light. You will cut gas usage 20 to 30 percent.

If you already have a gas stove, and it has a pilot light, turn it off. If you're in doubt about how to do it, have an appliance man show you how. The savings are worth it. Then get one of those decorative match holders for kitchen matches.

Another alternative to the gas stove pilot light is the flint lighter used with welding torches. It's easy to use, lights every time, and even saves the cost of matches.

when you fire it up. For instance, if you plan to bake pies, time it so you can cook an oven dinner in the same cycle.

Having roast beef or pork? Try baked acorn squash for the vegetable, and put some baked potatoes on the side. That way the whole meal can be oven-cooked in one shot, instead of firing up the stove burners, too.

Acorn squash is certainly not the only vegetable that will bake with a roast meat entree. Onions, beets, Hubbard squash, whole cauliflower, eggplant, sweet potatoes, turnips, and tomatoes are among the other tasty vegetables that can go in the oven. In addition, there are oven specialties like stuffed peppers, baked apples, glazed carrots, and that super-treat corn-on-the-cob baked in its own husks, or wrapped in foil.

Do you like mashed potatoes with your roast beef? My mother baked the potatoes; when they were done, she scooped them from their skins and mashed them. After mashing, they went back in the skins with a pat of butter and a little paprika on top, and back in the oven. Superb.

Casseroles are limited in their variety only by the extent of your imagination. Any time you are cooking cakes, pies, cookies, or even a roast, plan to cook a casserole at the same time. Start with cookbook recipes, and then get inventive on your own.

Before putting frozen foods in the oven, thaw them in the refrigerator or on the kitchen counter. They'll cook more quickly, therefore at less expense.

A small countertop oven-broiler can often be used for single casseroles or individual meals, and uses less electricity. With that appliance, plus the oven and oven-broiler in your stove, you'll have three choices. Use the smallest that will do the job.

After baking in the winter, leave the oven door open until the oven is cool. No sense wasting that heat. Conversely, in the summer try to schedule some of the baking for the cool of the evening, with obvious advantages.

Heat in the Kitchen

The heating units in electric appliances continue to radiate after being turned off. With a little practice you can learn to turn off the heat a few minutes early and finish with the leftover heat.

A pressure cooker uses much less fuel than a conventional pan. When preparing boiled potatoes, for instance, a pressure cooker will use 30 percent less energy, doing the job in half the time.

Quick cup of coffee? Your electric coffee pot will boil water more quickly at less cost than a pan on the stove.

Quick cup of instant soup? Chances are that hot water right from the faucet will turn the trick nicely without using the stove at all. The same trick will work with instant hot chocolate.

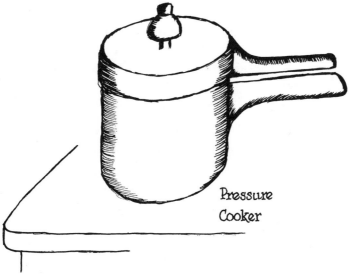

Pressure Cooker

The kitchen exhaust fan keeps the house cleaner, but in winter it is also pushing precious warm air into the outdoors. Some of the need for the exhaust fan results from the steam and grease spatters caused by cooking at higher temperatures than needed. An awareness of this situation can lead to twofold savings.

Retire That Appliance

Check the electrical appliances used in your kitchen. Individually the electric carving knife, electric can opener, electric mixer, electric peanut butter maker, electric sealer for plastic bags, electric sandwich grill, electric crepe maker, electric waffle iron, and the like don't use a lot of power, but taken together they're a considerable

THE APPETITES OF APPLIANCES

How much electricity do those appliances use, and how much do they cost us? A public utility furnished us these figures, and costs, which vary widely are based on a kwh charge of four cents. Change the cost figures to agree with the kwh charge shown on your recent utility bill.

Appliance	Average Wattage	kwh per Month	Cost per Month	Appliance	Average Wattage	kwh per Month	Cost per Month
Air conditioner	860	130	$5.20	Range			
Blanket	150	12.45	0.50	Small surface unit	1,300	10.4	0.42
Blender	386	0.19	0.01	Large	2,400	19.2	0.77
Clock	2	1.4	0.06	Self-cleaning			
Clothes dryer	4,856	83	3.32	(Once)	2,500	7.5	0.30
Coffee maker	600	7.5	0.30	Ref./freezer			
Cooker/fryer	1,200	2	0.08	(15 cubic feet)			
Dishwasher	1,200	30	1.20	Automatic	440	146	5.84
Freezer (14 cu. ft.)				Manual	325	94	3.76
Manual defrost	341	98	3.92	TV, B&W			
Automatic	440	146	5.84	Tube	160	29	1.16
Hair dryer				Solid state	55	10	0.40
Soft bonnet	400	2.5	0.10	TV, color			
Hard bonnet	900	3.83	0.15	Tube	300	55	2.20
Hand-held	600	2	0.08	Solid state	200	37	1.48
Heating system				Toaster	1,100	3.3	0.13
Burner motor	266	60	2.40	Toothbrush	1.1	0.8	0.03
Hot air fan	292	80	3.20	Washing machine			
Hot water circ.	120	30	1.20	Automatic	512	9	0.45
Humidifier	177	26	1.04	Non-automatic	286	6	0.24
Iron	1,100	5.72	0.23	Water Heater	3,000	405	16.20
Microwave oven	1,450	11.6	0.46	Qk. Rec.	4,500	405	16.20
Radio	71	7	0.28	Lighting	Var 80-150		3.20-6.00

drain over the year. There are easy, handy alternatives for all those things that use less power, or no power at all.

At our house, we don't include the electric toaster on that list of useless appliances. There's an outdoor camping toaster we can use with the wood stove. The electric toaster is still in use every day.

For desserts and snacks, consider goodies like sliced fresh peaches with milk and sugar, dried fruits, salted nuts, and the instant puddings that don't require cooking. Over the course of the year they'll be much more economical than pies and cakes that need to be baked.

Solving the Hot Water Problems

5

Solving the Hot Water Problems

Hot running water is one of the great inventions of modern civilization. Two hundred years ago only a minority of families in this country had indoor running water. One hundred years ago a minority had indoor hot running water.

Today, most homes have both hot and cold running water at the turn of the tap. With the increases in fuel prices, that's a mixed blessing. In many parts of the country, water itself is scarce and expensive. Everywhere, hot water costs more and more.

Hot water is important in three areas of the home: the kitchen, bathroom and laundry. They combine to make the water heater one of the major energy consumers in the home, whether your fuel is gas or electricity.

The hot water problem becomes entirely another matter when a full switch is made to wood heat or solar energy, and there are chapters on those matters for you to consider.

Let's say, though, that you're with the great majority: hot water available at the twist of the wrist from at least three faucets (it's seven at our house), serving one or more major appliances, and brought up to temperature by a gas or electric heater. You may well have bought this book because you knew you had a hot water problem. You're aware of it every time you pay the bills.

By the standards of former times, we all live like kings. That was fine when the project could be financed on an ordinary paycheck. More and more, though, the royal hot water at the fingertips demands at least a princely stipend, and you may have noticed that the regal treasury is straining at the demands made on it. This chapter is intended to help you scale down the use of this luxury from the level of imperial profligacy to a plateau of ducal pleasure.

There are proposals that can significantly alter the employment of hot water at your house, without uncomfortable sacrifice, and with resultant important savings. Let's get at it.

It's Dish-Washing Time

Yes, it's necessary to talk about washing dishes. The experts disagree on how hot the water should be in the household supply. Some say if you have an automatic dishwasher your water heater should be set at 150° F. Perhaps it should, if you have a need for something approaching sterilization. Otherwise, even with a dish-

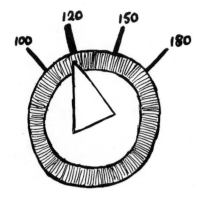

washer, 120° F. should be plenty hot enough. You can test it with a candy thermometer.

Is that temperature important? You bet. Heating water is the second greatest consumer of energy in the home, amounting to as much as 20 percent of the total domestic energy bill. Water being heated to more than 120° F. will need to be cooled again for almost all purposes, which is wasteful. Turn down the heater thermostat.

Whether you have a dishwasher, or do the dishes in the sink, an adequate supply of certain items will save fuel. You may not need two dozen pickle forks or three score demitasse cups, but it's a rare household that has too many spoons, coffee mugs, drinking glasses, or bowls. If you run short on these items constantly, buy an additional supply—maybe at the dime store—and you'll be running the hot water for dishwashing less often.

What is true for spoons and mugs is also true for saucepans and frypans. Having some extras of these items will mean you run the hot water for cleaning much less often.

With a dishwasher, letting dishes stack up till you have a full load every time is an important money saver. Grit your teeth and get used to it. Letting the dishes, pots, and pans pile up in the sink is much more economical than washing them a few at a time.

The most expensive way to rinse the dishes before putting them in the dishwasher is under a running hot water faucet. Next most expensive is in a sinkful of hot water. Best is in a sinkful of unheated tap water. Perhaps not too pleasant, but entirely effective.

If plates are crusted with breakfast egg, or a pan has beans burned on the bottom, let them soak for a few hours in unheated tap water. Nine times out of ten that will turn the trick at much less expense than a hot water soak, or scrubbing under a running faucet.

When shopping for a dishwasher, look for a model with a switch to cut off the automatic water heater and drying cycle. This will reduce energy consumption from one-third to one-half.

USE TWO SINKS

As a restaurant dishwasher years ago (I was working my way through college), I used two sinks: one for washing and one for rinsing. The rinsed dishes then went into a rack to air-dry. That's still the best and most economical way to do it. If you don't have a double sink, then a dishpan, big pot or mixing bowl on the counter will do for rinsing.

You already have a dishwasher without that feature? Well, when you can, watch the cycle dial. When it gets to the last air-dry segment, just turn it to stop and open the door. In the winter a little extra heat and humidity in the room will be helpful, and any time those hot dishes and pans will dry by themselves quite quickly.

Utensils that are used regularly for non-staining jobs like heating tea water and boiling eggs don't need to be washed. They can just be turned over in a sink rack and left to dry for the next use.

Incidentally, don't pour that hot water down the drain after boiling eggs or making spaghetti. Stopper the sink and leave the hot water in it for later washing chores, or just let it sit in the sink and cool. Letting the heat from the water radiate into the room makes more sense than heating a drain pipe.

Knives used for clean chores like cutting a grapefruit don't need the whole hot-water cleaning treatment. A quick splash under the cold water faucet and a wipe with a towel will do it. In fact, if you have good knives with riveted wooden handles, that cleaning method is much better for the knife than a hot water soaking.

If you have an undersink garbage disposer, flush it with cold water. You'll not only save energy, but the cold water will solidify the greases making them less likely to stick to the pipes and form a blockage.

Using the Bathroom

Let's take a trip to the john.

The invention of the single-action mixer faucet was a convenience breakthrough, but also a serious economy hazard. With that single-spout faucet you can get just the water temperature you want and let it run. Terrible. It would be better if you still had two separate faucets as your grandmother did. Then you'd need to stopper the sink and mix the right temperature in the bowl. Do it. You'll save money.

A GOOD LOCATION

In our house, we installed the dishwasher directly under the built-in oven and broiler. If you're building or remodeling you can tuck that one in the plans. The exhaust heat from the dishwasher rises to give a partial pre-heat to the ovens.

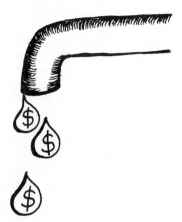

THAT DRIPPING FAUCET

Maybe you've seen how many gallons will drip through a leaky faucet in a year, and those figures haven't impressed you too much.

Maybe these will. In Pennsylvania, if a hot water faucet leaks one drop a second, the total cost in a year is $6.25 for the water and $8.70 to heat it. That's $14.95 gone down the drain.

That not only applies to that first face-washing to get the sleep out of your eyes, but also the male shaving chores, every time through on hand washing, rinsing out lingerie, and every bathroom use. With four folks in the house, each one using the bathroom sink, say, five times a day, just filling the sink instead of letting the water run might save as much as forty gallons a day in hot water. That's enough for two full loads through the washing machine, or three quick showers.

That quick shower takes about half as much hot water as a tub bath. Call soaking in the tub an occasional luxury, and the quick shower a frequent sanitary necessity.

When you take a tub bath, don't drain the water when you're through. Let the heat from the water radiate into the room until the water is cool. This, incidentally, is the basic principle of some of the solar heating systems. You might even stopper the tub when you take a shower, and let that hot water radiate its heat before it goes down the drain.

Be sure you turn off the faucet all the way when you're finished using sink or tub. If it still drips, ouch! One drop per second from a hot water faucet is 200 gallons a month, 2,400 gallons a year. An average water heater holds 40 gallons, so you can figure how much extra you're spending with the dripping faucet. Fix it.

Wash your hair when you shower. It won't get any cleaner with a separate washing in the sink, and the combination wash is a money-saver.

Cold Water for Your Laundry?

It's time to tackle the laundry.

Consider the cold water detergents. Only clothes that are very greasy need water as warm as 80° F. to get clean. Your washing machine probably has settings for cold, warm, and hot water. Use the cold for ordinary washing, the warm for very dirty clothes, the hot not at all. Your wash-and-wear clothes made with synthetic fibers will be just as clean and considerably less wrinkled

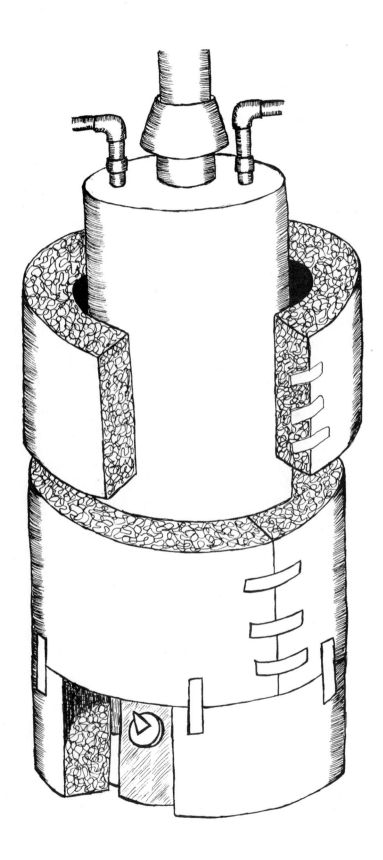

SIX WAYS TO CUT HOT WATER COSTS

Here are six ways you can cut the costs of heating water in your home.

1. Locate the water heater as near as possible to the places where hot water is used. Water cools as it makes a long trip through pipes.

2. Insulate the hot water pipes so they will retain more heat, particularly on those long runs of pipe.

3. Insulate the hot water pipes that travel through unheated areas and cold cellars. These are where insulating will be easiest. Both pipe insulation and wraparound insulation can be bought at most hardware stores and is simple to install.

4. Pad the water heater with batts of the six-inch fiberglass insulation that's used in ceilings. The cost of this will be about $6, and your savings will pay for it quickly.

5. If yours is an electric water heater, check with the power company about an off-peak meter. This means your heater will operate at times when the company has power to spare, and you can buy at a lower rate.

6. The water heater has a drain valve at the bottom. Use it about twice a year, or oftener if there is considerable sediment in your water supply. Draining the heater will flush out that sediment, allowing the heating elements to operate much more efficiently.

SEPARATE THERMOSTATS?

A final suggestion for the kitchen, bath and laundry areas: If possible, have each of them on a separate thermostat and keep those thermostats at a low setting—as low as 50° F. in the laundry, and 60° F. in the bath and kitchen. These rooms get plenty warm when in use, so why heat them when they're not being used?

if you use cold water for washing. And by using cold water washing techniques you'll save $5-$10 a month in hot water costs. With today's detergents, cold water rinsing is fully effective, and the rinse cycles are probably half of the water you use in washing.

Running your washing machine for just a few items? Wasteful. Perhaps it's because some of the necessary items in the household are in short supply, so you're washing more often than you need to. Stock up at least a week's supply of the commonplace, most-used items like socks and underwear. It's cheaper to have enough for each person so use of the washing machine can be less frequent.

A larger supply of the frequently washed clothes will also allow better use of the different washing cycles with full loads. Lightweight items such as underclothes, handkerchiefs, blouses, and pillowcases can take a shorter cycle than heavyweights like blankets, jackets, and dirty towels. Have a sufficient supply so you can make up full, separate loads of the different kinds of washes you do.

Your conscience may call for the hot water sterilization treatment for some things like baby clothes. Have enough of these, too, so you can make up full loads and make the most of the hot water you use.

When shopping for a new washing machine, look for the versatility of partial-load washing for those times when you'll need it, and for the ability to wash at different temperatures. Beyond that, be skeptical of over-fussy controls and multiple cycles. All that electronic gadgetry runs with electric current and spins the meter.

6

Save With Solar

It's a reasonable guess that by the turn of the century most of the new homes built in our country will be designed to make effective use of solar energy.

Between now and then, many existing homes will be retrofitted with various kinds of solar energy devices. Gradually the cost of these devices will come down as they go into mass production, and their efficiency will increase at the same time.

The move to solar energy has already begun. Today there are hundreds of homes fitted with solar energy systems; within a year or two there will be thousands. The first step for many folks will be a solar energy hot water system. Such systems are now available either for new homes or for retrofitting on older homes. They will furnish from 80 to 100 percent of the hot water requirements with fuel costs ranging from zero to very modest for a standby system to take over in an extended period of very cloudy weather.

If you've gotten that far into the employment of solar energy, maybe you don't need to read this chapter. You're already well acquainted with the principles involved.

On the other hand, if a solar energy system is still some distance into the future for you, read on. There will be some ideas here you can use.

To start with, you're already using solar energy.

Each window on the south side of your house is, or can be, a quite effective solar energy collector. I'm not talking about some new development by which you can make your house look like a space station on "Star-Trek." I'm talking about plain, old-fashioned windows.

Sun heat is obviously present on every clear day. Not so obviously, the warmth of the sun is still with us on cloudy days. In fact, the hours of daylight even on a dim day have something to offer in reducing your fuel bills.

If you get intrigued with the solar possibilities, there are books and plans available that will take you beyond the scope of this chapter. We hope herein to offer some suggestions; some things you can do right away, at minimal cost and effort, to take greater advantage of that great free source of energy, the sun.

Use Solar Heat—Now

Don't think of solar heat as something for the future, in a new home. Make use of it now. Here are some ways to do it.

• Taking advantage of the sun's heat begins on the outside of your house. Black and other dark colors absorb sun warmth; white and light colors reflect that warmth. Assuming you live where it gets cold in the winter, dark colors for your house exterior, and particularly your roof, will pass through more of the available heat from the sun.

• You can get sunburned under water; you can get sunburned on a cloudy day; you can get sunburned through a T-shirt; you can get sunburned on a ski slope when the temperature is below zero. Naturally, the windows of your house, and especially those facing south, can pass through a lot of sun heat.

• Storm windows impede the passage of sun heat very little, but they do keep in the heat once it has entered your house. That's the principle of the greenhouse, where summertime flowers can be grown in the dead of winter.

LEARNING THE HOT WAY

Along with a bunch of other guys, I not only had most of the skin peel off my nose and cheekbones, but also got a painful sunburn across the shoulders right through the jacket of some Army work clothes. We were in basic training at a southern post and spent two full days, dawn to dusk, unshaded in a field exercise. I've had an educated respect for sun power ever since.

• One of the concepts in use in complete solar energy systems is the heat collector. This is often a bed of sand or rocks under a house, or a large mass of water, in which sun heat can be stored. You can take advantage of this concept by having solid objects standing in the sunlight to store warmth that will be radiated after the sun goes down.

• One good heat collector is a windowsill row of flowerpots, or an indoor windowbox. The earth in pots or box will store warmth during the day with the double advantage of helping the plants to grow and warming the room at night.

• Another good heat collector is a stone or concrete floor. You probably have such a floor down cellar. Consider cutting through a south window to let the winter sun permeate that solid surface, making a free radiator.

• Will the low-lying winter sun slant across the room to warm a brick-fronted fireplace, a slate entryway, or a similar solid surface? Be sure the drapes are pulled back to take advantage of this solar collector.

• Light-colored shades or slatted blinds drawn across a sunny window will reflect the sun warmth right back outdoors again. During the daylight hours, keep the sunny windows in the clear to let that sun warmth in.

• If you have unused space up under your roof—and this will certainly be true if yours is a newer house with a truss-roof design—consult with a plumber on the cost of putting an old-style, second-hand, uninsulated hot water tank up there. At least during the warmer months, the upstairs tank, linked in the water lines before the water gets to your regular heater, will pre-heat the water, making less work and less fuel usage for household hot water.

• If your roof is insulated, rather than your attic floor, that up-top waste space will be warmer than outdoors even in winter, so the tank up there can be an advantage in pre-warming your water all year-round.

• Sunshine is not only a source of warmth, but also, of course, a source of light at the same time. Flicking on the light switches in the daytime may be a habit you can break just by rearranging the furniture.

• Next time you're ready to repaint or repaper a room, think about how the room is used before you choose the colors. Light colors in a room will bounce the daylight around, making it a pleasant and cheerful place without extra illumination. This is a much less important factor in bedrooms, which are used primarily at night.

• In fact, in rooms used solely for sleeping the only advantage windows have is for a little ventilation. Wintertime solar heat just isn't available when the room is in use, so let the windows be small, or heavily draped.

• Window light in the kitchen is a tough problem, because you want a lot of storage, rather than windows, on those outside walls. Even more important, then, are the light colors for those kitchen walls.

GRANDMA UNDERSTOOD

My grandmother's house had two shades on each window: one in a light ivory color and the other a dark green. Each had neighborly modesty as the primary function, I suppose, but the light shades were pulled in the summer to reflect out unwanted heat; the dark shades in winter to let in heat. The lace curtains were just to look pretty. The grandfolks may not have known the sophisticated principles of solar energy, but they did know what worked.

• If you're designing from scratch, or doing a major remodeling, think about a combined kitchen-dining area with storage on the north wall and windows on south and east walls. That way you can have both storage and sunshine.

• Daytime reading and working areas can be placed where window light will be sufficient on all but the darkest, overcast days. Specifically, consider the location of the sewing machine, the chair with the magazine rack, the playtable for the children, the workbench, as well as more obvious items like the artist's easel and the author's typewriter.

• If you have dark but useful rooms in the attic, consider putting skylights in the roof. Installing a skylight is considerably less complicated and expensive than building a dormer, and will change a gloomy cave needing artificial light into a pleasant place that's less expensive to use.

That attic skylight should be a double-paned thermal window, or the heat loss in winter will much more than cancel out the savings you gain from the daylight.

Some direct uses of solar energy are available to you. A double-paned window is a kind of solar transfer system. In another chapter we mention a window greenhouse for growing vegetables in the winter. That window greenhouse will also be a source of daytime warmth for the room where it is installed.

One of the newer developments available for many homeowners is the solar room—a considerable step ahead of the window greenhouse, but less expensive than a full-scale greenhouse.

• The solar room, of course, will do best if you build it on a south wall of your house. The next best choice is an east wall.

• Your solar room will gather heat even during overcast winter days. You'll have the most advantage from it when there are practical ways for you to conduct that heat to the rest of the house. Consider a simple duct and register system to let the extra heat flow upstairs without the need of electric blowers.

• There will be a natural daytime/nighttime temperature variation in your solar room, so grow the hardier plants and vegetables, avoiding the exotic tropicals that would require supplementary heat.

• Going to build a solar room? You'll have more advantage from it when the back wall is a dark color to absorb sun warmth.

• You'll add another dimension to your solar room benefits when the back wall is not only dark, but a solid masonry like concrete or stone that will retain sun heat into the nighttime hours.

Here is some miscellaneous information that may encourage you to go the solar way:

• Adding a window of conventional size—about two feet by five feet—on the south side of your house can provide as much heat as five to fifteen gallons of oil, provided it is tightly sealed against the winds, and draped at night.

• That window will save an additional three to fourteen gallons of oil each winter if it has a storm window.

• That same window will save from five to twenty-five gallons of oil each winter if you install double storm windows on it, adding up to three thicknesses of glass. With oil figured at a low forty cents a gallon, that's a total combined saving for the new window with double storm windows of somewhere between $4 and $16 a year.

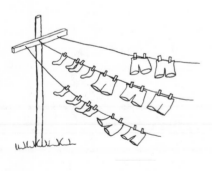

• Finally, don't forget the simplest solar energy device of them all, the solar clothes drier. It works like a charm. It's also called the famous backyard rope clothesline, and it will save you at least $50 a year.

Good News in Your Garden

7

Good News in
Your Garden

Nationally, one of the major consumers of energy is agri-business.

Once upon a time, food was raised with methods that the economists call "labor-intensive." Today, American food-raising is very clearly "energy-intensive." Petroleum-based herbicides, pesticides, and fertilizers are spread on the American farmlands by a variety of fascinating machines, including the romantic crop-dusting airplanes. Planting, cultivating, and harvesting are all accomplished with more sophisticated machines.

Food products are processed in factories, refrigerated, trucked across the country, and then displayed in your supermarket, often in refrigerated cases. Every step of the way, energy is being consumed.

In fact, for almost everything you buy at the store, the fuel bill accounts for more of the price tag than the product itself. That's why growing your own fruits and vegetables can be a substantial money-saver.

Your own garden is "labor-intensive," in the manner of food-growing since the earliest days. The hand methods that are no longer practical on the commercial farms are still very effective in your backyard.

Just as you may have a power mower for your lawn, you will want a power tiller if your vegetable garden is of any size. This is a long way from the gallon-gulpers you see pictured on the big agri-spreads. Neither the mower nor the tiller is going to bankrupt you at the gas pump, particularly if you keep their engines tuned for efficient operation.

The secret to making your food garden a real money-saver isn't in the growing of the food itself, it's in the preserving for year-round use on your table. An "eating garden" is mostly for fun and because you like fresh corn and tomatoes in season. The real saving is when you have nutritious, garden-grown edibles in the off seasons. Your garden can save more than $1,000 a year for a household of four, studies have shown.

Some practical food-preserving methods use no fuel at all, and other, sometimes easier, methods use little energy. Then there are the "energy-intensive" methods, like freezing. As in other aspects of your living, there are choices and compromises.

Food is one of the necessities, obviously; not one of life's options. At the market, $70 a week comes to more than $3,500 a year. Some of that market cost, for such items as pepper, matches, and toilet paper, will continue no matter how ingenious you are in your garden, and the miracles of modern science have yet to produce the pork chop tree. The estimate, though, that you can save about one-third of that bill by food gardening at home is a modest projection.

Is the garden worth the effort? Since this is a book about saving money, that's a valid question.

Well, figuring a little less than a half-hour a day for thirteen weeks of the growing season, about ten hours to get ready and plant, about thirty hours to harvest and preserve, and a final six hours to put your garden to bed for the season, $1,000 worth of harvest is the equivalent of paying yourself about $11 an hour. You can decide if that's worth the effort.

More From Your Garden

Let's consider ways you can get more—and store more—from your garden.

The traditional rows of garden vegetables look very

WE OVERPLANT

In our garden we have enough space to overplant, that is to plant more than we need. That way we can lose a little to the weeds, and a little more to hungry wildlife, and still do not have a disaster at harvest time.

Some folks put up an electric fence to keep out the critters; we feel we don't need one.

orderly and are well adapted to machine cultivation. Actually, though, they demand a lot more work than is necessary. Many vegetables such as peas, beans, and leaf lettuce, do much better when planted in beds instead of in rows. Chards, spinach, beets, and carrots also take well to bed-planting instead of row-planting. The advantage is less time with the tiller because the beds require less cultivation through the growing season. And of course there's a great saving in space. Try a seedbed two to four feet wide. You'll soon learn how to sprinkle the seeds for proper spacing.

Beets and particularly carrots are very slow getting started. Mix some radish seeds in with each of these. The early radishes will mark the bed, and as you pull them up for eating they will make room for the carrots and beets.

When picking your harvest, do a little kitchen work before you go in the house. Corn husks, tops of radishes and carrots, pea shucks and other throwaways can be left right in the garden plot. They will return to the soil and help to nourish it without artificial fertilizers. This is particularly important if you have been accustomed to grinding these things down the drain through the garbage disposal unit.

Save paper bags. When you go to the garden to harvest, take a recycled bag with you. Do the preliminary preparation there in the garden plot, and bring a bag of ready vegetables into the house.

When planning your garden, think of storing crops without wasting energy. Winter squash, onions, corn, carrots, turnips, parsnips, kidney beans, and potatoes all can be stored without canning or freezing.

Drying and Storing

Peel back the husks on ears of corn, but don't tear them off. With about half the husks, braid three ears together and hang them on the wall or in the attic. The kernels will dry, and can be renewed months later for eating by soaking them overnight in water or milk. The kernels taken from three good-sized ears will make a side dish for four at the table.

Dried corn can also be ground into cornmeal. Either soaked for serving, or fresh-ground for mush or baking, the dried corn is sweet and delicious.

Onions can be braided by their dried tops and hung to dry. When it's time to use them they'll be just like the ones you buy at the store, with dried layers on the outside and a tasty onion inside.

In the spring, dried onions are inclined to obey their natural impulses and start sprouting. Don't fight it. The first scallions will be along in the garden in a few weeks. The sprouting can be minimized by putting the onions in the refrigerator.

Winter squashes will store for as long as six months in a cool place, with no loss in flavor or nutrient value. Leave them outdoors in the fall to harden their skins before storing them. It's best to have them off the ground for that hardening process.

Where's a cool place? Old-time farm homes had what was called a **root cellar.** Often it was separate from the house, dug into an earth-bank, or set into a pit in the ground. You can set aside a corner of your cellar for a cool room, put up walls, and insulate them. There's a double advantage: You not only have a convenient, no-cost vegetable storage, but it's also a section of the house you don't need to pay to heat.

Potatoes, apples, pears, quinces, carrots, beets, parsnips, and turnips will store well in the cool room. Check with a good book on food preserving for the appropriate methods.

If underground, or well insulated in your cellar, your cool room will maintain a fairly constant 45° F. all year-round. That's about the same temperature as your refrigerator, which means it isn't suitable for long storage of meats, but will cool beverages to a pleasant chill for summer enjoyment.

Navy beans, lima beans, peas, and kidney beans can be dried easily for storage. Let them ripen on the vine and begin drying in the pod, then spread them on cloths

SAVE THOSE ZUCCHINIS

Zucchini is a notoriously prolific crop. Most people who plant zucchini and other summer squashes are overwhelmed with a larger harvest than they can handle. One answer is freezing some for later use, but a less energy-expensive answer is to let them grow to full size. We tried it and discovered that the outer husk will get quite hard on the mature fruit, and it will store in a cool place for as long as three months. It must be peeled before eating, and it can be either boiled or fried.

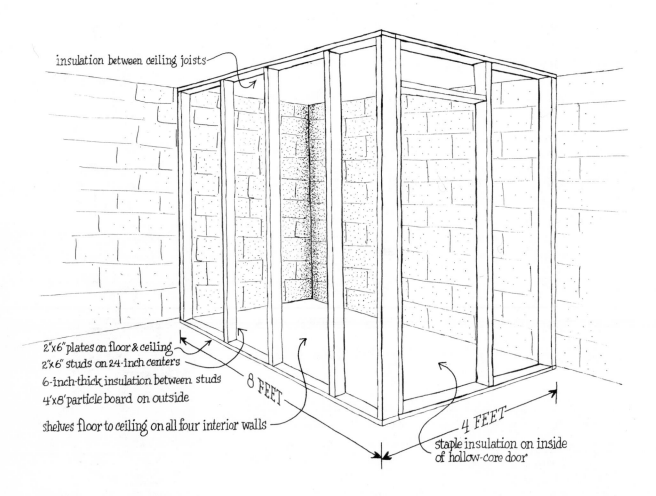

insulation between ceiling joists

2"x6" plates on floor & ceiling
2"x6" studs on 24-inch centers
6-inch-thick insulation between studs
4'x8' particle board on outside

shelves floor to ceiling on all four interior walls

8 FEET

4 FEET

staple insulation on inside
of hollow-core door

SUGARING

We boil off maple syrup early every spring. Our rig isn't fancy; just a big washtub on an outdoor fireplace. In preparation for the event, some days the preceding fall are spent gathering up the broken branches, trimmed-out saplings and other junk wood around the place. These are stacked and ready for sugaring, minimizing the fuel costs and getting the yard cleaned up at the same time.

(that's what you were saving that torn sheet for) to finish drying in the sun. When the drying process is complete, pack in jars for later use.

Apple slices, carrot strips, and many other fruits and vegetables can be dried for storage. What you need is a book on food preserving.

Home dehydrators will speed up the drying process, and you may need one, considering how uncertain the sunshine can be at the end of the growing season. Look for maximum fuel economy. The models differ considerably in their fuel efficiency.

Efficient Ways to Can

After cool storage and drying, canning is the most energy-efficient. This has nothing to do with cans. Canning is putting up foods in glass jars, which must be sterilized by boiling. When you have a wood stove, you'll make out best in fuel efficiency, because you can bake in the oven and cook stovetop meals in the same cycle as your canning.

Canning efficiency is increased as your batches get bigger. Get a production line going, so that when one batch of jars and lids is sterilized, you're ready to use them and put in the next batch.

Canning is the most efficient way to keep tomatoes, the preferred way for pickles, and the only way for jams, jellies, and maple syrup, so get hip to the canning method.

Shelf space in a coolish place is mandatory for keeping the product of your canning efforts. That probably isn't on shelves over the refrigerator, where exhaust heat from the refrigerator motor creates extra warmth. See if there is room for shelves along the cellar stairs—the old-timer's favorite spot for canned goods—out in the garage, or in your cool room. Don't expose your canned goods to freezing temperatures.

GOOD EATING AHEAD

With the fresh vegetables from your indoor gardening efforts you not only will have taste and nutrition for your table, but also you'll have food that doesn't need cooking, right through the winter.

Here's a menu for you: creamed dried beef on boiled potatoes with lettuce and tomatoes on the side. You can dry the beef and keep it in jars, store the potatoes in your cool room, and grow the lettuce and tomatoes in pots.

Here's another: stuffed peppers with baked onions and glazed carrots. You can grow the peppers in pots indoors, hang the onions to dry, and store the carrots in a sand barrel. Add some hamburger for the pepper stuffing and you can cook this dinner all at once in the oven. Good show.

FREEZING: EASY BUT EXPENSIVE

The easiest way to preserve foods from your garden is by freezing them. But remember, it uses and uses energy.

For freezing foods, most of the textbooks recommend blanching for various periods of time before the foods go into the freezer container. Blanching is a partial pre-cooking; that is, dipping the foods in boiling water, then cooling them in ice water. Again, getting set with the largest batch recommended will mean that the boiling water is on the fire for the minimum possible time.

Remember, at the other end of the cycle, to take the foods from the freezer a half-hour or so before cooking time, or pre-thaw them in the refrigerator. They'll need less cooking time that way.

And another repeat note: A full freezer takes less electricity to operate. As your supply of food diminishes toward the end of the winter, it will save on fuel bills if you fill paper or plastic milk containers with water and freeze them just to keep the freezer full. You may find that during the summer those blocks of ice are just what you want for cooling a tub full of punch, or for chilling the portable cooler chest.

If there is cupboard space in your kitchen for your supply of canned goods, let it be in an enclosed place where nothing else is stored. With the cupboard doors opened only for taking out foods at mealtimes, the space will stay cool, which is good for the canned goods, and also is one more chunk of space you don't need to pay to heat.

Indoor Gardening

Don't be satisfied with cornpone, dried beans, and jerky beef for those winter meals. An important part of the good news from your garden is that you can have a garden indoors for those salad greens.

Leaf lettuce is easy to grow in pots or windowsill boxes. Consider putting an extra-wide sill on one of your big south-facing windows, and filling the sill with eating plants. The humidity they will add to the room will be welcome in winter, and they will give you salads every day while others are paying those high prices for long-distance lettuce.

Another expedient is to install a set of shelves across that south window, to increase your indoor garden growing room.

You can grow fresh spinach, chives, parsley and other herbs in windowsill pots or growing boxes. The flats you may use for starting bedding plants in the spring won't do for this purpose. The soil is too shallow for good root growth, and the shallow seedbed will be a nuisance for needing to be watered too often. Let your growing soil be as deep as you can manage conveniently.

Tomatoes and green peppers can be grown successfully in indoor pots. The little globes called cherry tomatoes are recommended. Both tomatoes and peppers require a substantial amount of soil for best growth—about a bucketful per plant, which suggests that one kind of pot to use is an ordinary bucket.

Red clay pots can be almost as big as buckets, and they are a bit more decorative. Don't try to hide these

OUR INDOOR GARDEN

We had a spot that was made to order for an experiment in indoor gardening: a set of south windows at ground level with a concrete wall and floor. I made a waist-high seedbed out of scrap wood, lined it with polyethylene sheeting, filled it with dirt, and hung a fluorescent fixture over it for supplementary light. By watering just once a week, we've had champion crops of leaf lettuce with a continuous harvest from October till March, and similar success with parsley, chives, and (hold your hat) celery.

vegetables. Put them right out in the room by that sunny south window. As their fruits mature, they will be a bright and colorful touch in the room.

The tomato plants will need some help to pollinate and as the fruit matures. Use sections of broomstick jammed deep into the dirt to stake them up. When blossoms appear, snap the stems with one finger daily, to start the fruiting process. Strips of cloth for tying are less likely to bruise the stems than lengths of cord. Use red ribbons with big bows if you like to have fun in your house.

Cold Frames
and Greenhouses

More traditional for fresh vegetables in the winter is the outdoor cold frame, which in the older time was an unused glass storm window placed over a box sunk into the

INDOOR BROCCOLI

I haven't seen broccoli recommended for indoor growing, but I've tried it and had it work out with little effort. If your luck goes like mine you won't get big heads of broccoli, but you will keep on getting tender little heads as long as you keep cutting it before the flowers bloom. In midwinter when fresh broccoli costs a fortune at the store, it's good to be eating your own.

earth. Even in the northernmost states, you can count on salad greens for Thanksgiving dinner from a cold frame that has required almost no effort.

• A somewhat more elaborate application of the same principle is the sun-heated greenhouse developed by Scott and Helen Nearing. It furnishes them with fresh vegetables right through the winter months. They've written a book about it, **Building and Using Our Sun-Heated Greenhouse.** Read it.

• Yet another alternative is the window greenhouse, a cheery design whether or not you plan to grow vegetables. It provides many times the space of a windowsill, with the simplest kind of construction. There are commercial brands available for various sized windows; detailed plans can be purchased if you want to build it yourself. It's easy.

• Go the whole route. Build a solar room. You'll find it described in the chapter on solar energy.

• A separate greenhouse of commercial design, or even one attached to your house, may not give you a net energy saving. Heating one is expensive, and electrically operated temperature and humidity controls may run up the bill, too. Without those controls, you'd need to be in hourly attendance, adjusting shades, opening vents, and spraying mists.

The Wood Fuel Trip

8

8

The Wood Fuel Trip

As the prices for conventional fuels steadily rise, more and more folks are considering the possibility of burning wood at home. Smart move.

One scientific estimate has it that there is enough fuel wood available in the nation to heat more than half of the homes. What's so good about that is the self-renewing nature of our potential wood fuel supply. It's not just that there's enough fuel wood for half the homes this year; that's enough for half the homes every year.

To say it another way, America's present forest lands produce about thirteen billion cubic feet of potential fuel wood each year. Were we to put our minds to it in cultivating and harvesting, we might be well able to increase that amount by as much as 50 percent in ten years.

Getting that down to personal terms, a well-managed woodlot no bigger than twelve acres will provide enough fuel for an average home, every year, forever.

If you have a fireplace, you can start taking advantage of the wood fuel supply. You should know that a fireplace is an inefficient way to burn wood, and requires some managing just to give you a net heat gain. We'll explain that a little later. Even so, a fireplace is a start.

In fact, a fireplace can be a fine start, because it means you have a chimney available, which is one of the essentials for using wood as fuel. There are a number of good wood stove models that are designed to fit on your fireplace hearth and be vented up the fireplace chimney, so if you get at all serious about wood fuel, a fireplace can be a substantial beginning.

It can be helpful to know what are the better kinds of wood to burn. Locked in a hickory log, for instance, is twice as much potential heat as in a butternut log of exactly the same size. When looking for fuel efficiency, this kind of knowledge can be very helpful, and it's outlined in the pages that follow.

Much of the wood-burning wisdom goes back to the very dawn of civilization, because wood was the original fuel, and, in fact, was the dominant fuel in use in the United States as recently as 150 years ago. The tools, equipment, and know-how for using wood fuel are all readily available, both because there are many homes where wood has always been used for heating, and many more where the roofs are sprouting shiny new chimneys.

Incidentally, we don't plan to get into the details of wood stove installation and maintenance, which is the province of other volumes, but we feel compelled to offer one caution. By its very nature, an open fire in your home can be dangerous, and there are particular hazards inherent in the chimneys of fireplaces and woodstoves.

Splitting Axe

Before installing a stove get some expert advice, or consult an authoritative book on the subject. We'd hate to think that your reading of this chapter had created an enthusiasm that placed the security of your home in jeopardy.

About any way you use wood fuel, you're going to get some exercise. At the very least, you'll be carrying logs to the fireplace, or sticks to the stove, and later getting the ashes into a bucket or scuttle for removal. The exercise scale goes all the way from those modest chores to full management of a woodlot and felling your own trees. Where you want to be on that scale will depend on how much you like working outdoors, and how much employment you think your muscles need.

Every part of the wood fuel process you do yourself will save you money. Where I live, for instance, a cord of wood split, delivered, and stacked in yard or garage, will cost $60 to $85. It takes about seven cords to heat my house for the winter, so getting my fuel that way could cost almost $600, which would be cheaper than running the oil burner. However, I can cut it myself in the State Forest for just $3 a cord, and I can cut it on my own land for nothing.

I have bought wood already split; I have bought wood ready for splitting; and I have cut my own. What I do depends in part on my available time when the woodpile needs replenishing. For a cheery fireplace, or a complete wood heat system, you'll likely make your decisions that same way.

Open up the damper and fire the kindling. Here we go.

A More Efficient Fireplace

You have a fireplace? Let's start there.

• A fireplace is likely to steal more heat than it delivers. The necessary draft up the chimney pulls warm air from the room, resulting in a net heat loss. This is particularly

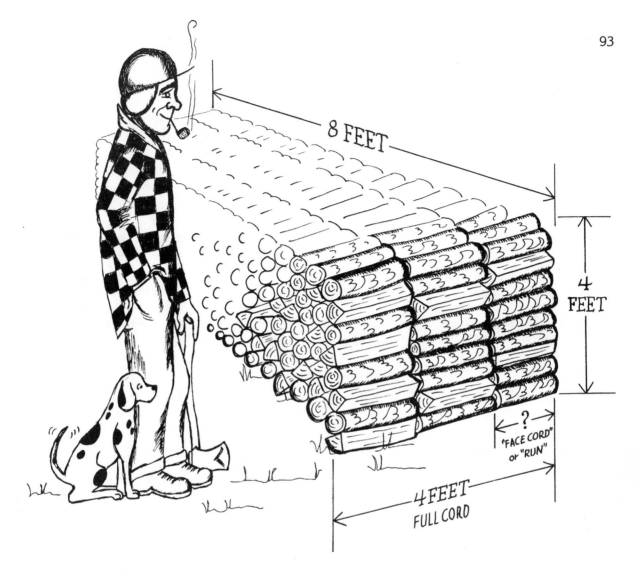

true as the fire is dying down, radiating less heat into the room, but still having a good draft up the chimney.

• Your fireplace should have a damper, a gate that closes off the chimney at the throat of the fireplace. As soon as a fire is out and no longer smoking, the damper should be closed. An open fireplace damper will drain heat from a house as fast as an open window.

• Glass doors on your fireplace will let you see the flames, while minimizing the heat loss from the room. They are particularly valuable after you've gone to bed, leaving a dying fire, because they cut off the heat loss from the room as the fire dies.

FIREPLACE DOORS

A friend of mine had steel doors made and hung them on the brick front of his fireplace. He could then enjoy the relaxation of the open fire during the quiet evening hours, and use his woodburner like a well-made stove the rest of the time. He says it works fine.

• Another compromise is the Franklin stove (which bears little resemblance to anything inventor Ben Franklin ever designed). You can open the cast-iron doors to enjoy the open fire, then close them at all other times to achieve something like a closed, cast-iron box stove.

• There are many makers of Franklin stoves, and some are better than others. The cheapest ones are likely to have a cast-iron front and top, and sheet metal sides and back. This is less desirable. A cast-iron model is best.

• Some of the Franklin models are designed to sit on your fireplace hearth and be vented up the fireplace chimney. A worthwhile idea. One model has an additional door on the side for firing the stove while the front doors are shut. This model also has an interior baffle system for greater fuel efficiency. Look for it.

• If you're planning to build a fireplace, consider including a sheet metal "heatilator" box. It will draw in cool air from the floor, warm it around the firebox, and send it warm into the room from vents. By combining it with a glass screen, you can have a modicum of heat efficiency this way.

• Another fireplace accessory is the hollow-tube grate. This is a set of metal pipes open at both ends, used instead of andirons. The pipes are shaped with their lower ends facing the room near floor level. The pipes run back across the bottom of the fireplace, and up the back of the firebox, and the upper ends are aimed out into the room again. As the fire heats, a draft is created in the pipes, picking up cooler air at floor level, warming it, and sending it back to the room as warm air. Some of the models are augmented with an electric blower. You can decide for yourself whether you like the way it looks.

• The greatest heat loss from a fireplace may be during the night, after an evening fire, when the damper must remain open to let out the smoke. Covering the fireplace

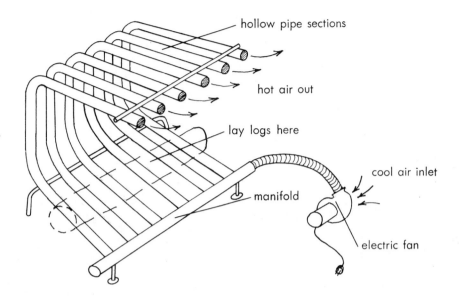

hollow pipe sections

hot air out

lay logs here

cool air inlet

manifold

electric fan

opening with a sheet of asbestos millboard or aluminum will cut off this flow of heated air up the chimney.

Speaking of Wood

Let's talk about wood.

The accompanying charts show the actual fuel values in various types of wood. The differences are significant. In some areas the fuel woods of lesser value are more readily available, and everywhere pine is easier to cut and split than beech. Get acquainted with what burns best and longest among the woods available where you live.

There's another diagram describing the actual dimensions of that mysterious measurement, the cord. Because so many homeowners don't know what a full cord is, the woodseller can often get away with selling what he loosely calls a cord of wood that is really precisely what he felt like throwing on the truck that day. Knowing can be saving.

CHOOSING FIREWOOD

1. THE GOOD WOODS

Tree	BTU's per cord (in 000's)
Shagbark Hickory	24,600
Black Locust	24,600
Ironwood (Hardhack)	24,100
Apple	23,877
Rock Elm	23,488
White Oak	22,700
Beech	21,800
Yellow Birch	21,300
Sugar Maple	21,300
Red Oak	21,300
White Ash	20,000

Several of these best-burning trees would rarely be cut for firewood. White oak, yellow birch, and sugar maple are valuable for furniture-making. You might cut one with a rotten core or mis-shapen trunk for firewood, and the limbs of these trees when full grown can be cut up into good lengths for burning. Also check for scrapwood at a furniture factory.

Hardhack is considered a trash tree where I live. It's not any good for furniture-making or pulpwood for papermaking, and it grows prolifically. I've never seen a big one. The small ones that I cut out when I'm clearing a plot make fine firewood, as the roster indicates.

Apple trees incline to be gnarled and tough when full grown. You'll have few long lengths to cut and split, and plenty of knots. However, they have a most pleasant aroma while burning, and you may decide that apple is worth struggling with for that reason.

Elm has a very irregular grain; yellow birch has a very tight grain; both are tough to split. Oak, ash, and maple all split much more easily.

2. SECOND-CHOICE WOODS

Tree	BTU's per cord (in 000's)
Black Walnut	19,500
White Birch	18,900
Black Cherry	18,770
Tamarack (Larch)	18,650
Red Maple	18,600
Green Ash	18,360
Pitch Pine	17,970
Sycamore	17,950
Black Ash	17,300
American Elm	17,200
Silver Maple	17,000

If there's a straight stretch of trunk as much as four feet long on either a black walnut or a black cherry tree, you'd be a fool to cut it into firewood. These are highly prized for making furniture veneers, and should be sold to a specialty mill. As with oak, birch, and maple, the branches and trimmings from walnut and cherry make dandy firewood for either stove or fireplace.

White birch is the one with the waterproof bark and must be split within weeks of cutting or it will start to rot.

Pitch pine has the BTUs for burning, but as its name indicates, it will put a deposit of pitch in your chimney, increasing the possibility of a chimney fire.

Again, elm is tough to split; maple and ash are easier splitting, and white birch is usually a joy to split. With any of them, when you have a big chunk from near the bottom of the tree, don't try to split it down the middle. Lop off easier sections from around the outside until it's trimmed down to a manageable size for a center cut.

3. HARDLY WORTHWHILE CUTTING

Tree	BTU's per cord (in 000's)
Red Spruce	13,632
Hemlock	13,500
Black Willow	13,206
Butternut	12,800
Red Pine	12,765
Aspen (Poplar)	12,500
White Pine	12,022
Basswood	11,700
Balsam Fir	11,282

You'll note that in this group of low-value woods is a concentration of the evergreens. If you're looking for a quick generality, stay away from the evergreens. Not only are they low in thermal values, but they will gum up your chimney.

There are some pretty Christmas trees here. Comparing the BTU values, though, you'll get almost twice as much warmth in your home from the woods on List 1.

Because they have, in general, looser grains, some of these low-value woods will split more easily. Also, a tight cord in these woods will only weigh about half as much as the good woods. Go for the heavy woods with the tight grains. You'll get much more heating value for your money and effort.

Burning fresh-cut wood will deposit creosote in your chimney that can result in a chimney fire. You'll run less risk and need to clean your chimney less often if you always burn wood that has been cut and split at least six months.

You can be sure you're burning dry wood when your home supply is stacked at least six months before you intend to use it.

Stacking wood in the side yard? Put down parallel poles with the bark still on and stack on top of them. Eventually they will rot, but that's better than having the ground rot eat away firewood into which you've put the work of cutting and splitting.

Split Your Own Wood

• Think about buying your firewood unsplit. It will be less expensive that way. Good exercise, too, and a splendid way to work out your hostilities.

• Splitting wood on the concrete floor in cellar or garage, or on a brick or stone hearth, is a sure way to ruin your axe, no matter how careful you think you can be.

• Some wavy-grained woods like ash don't split worth a darn. Birch and maple split beautifully. A piece of gnarled cherry is another tough one. Choose your firewoods with this in mind, if you're going to do the splitting.

• Don't try to split long sections of wood before cutting them into stove or fireplace lengths. Do the cutting first. Short lengths split much more easily.

• For splitting firewood, a somewhat dull axe is better than one with a razor edge. There's not only less risk of cutting yourself, but also less chance of getting the axe stuck in the wood.

Buck Saw

GETTING THE WOOD SUPPLY

I do some of my wood-cutting in the spring, as soon as the snow melts down far enough to make walking in the woods possible, and before the underbrush begins to grow. Trimming and cutting to length are done in the garden plot. The resulting twigs and small branches are piled and burned. Then the ashes and sawdust are tilled under to enrich my garden soil.

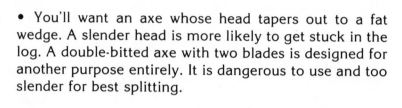

• Hold the axe handle as near to the end as you can comfortably and take a full swing. That way the momentum weight of the axe-head will be doing the work, instead of just your muscle power.

• You'll want an axe whose head tapers out to a fat wedge. A slender head is more likely to get stuck in the log. A double-bitted axe with two blades is designed for another purpose entirely. It is dangerous to use and too slender for best splitting.

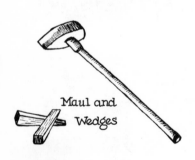

Maul and Wedges

• For splitting big, knotty lengths of wood, a maul or a sledgehammer and some splitting wedges will turn the trick. A maul looks like a sledge with one side tapered to an edge. Splitting wedges look like fat slices of pie made from tempered steel.

• If you're going to get into splitting a year's supply of fuel wood for your home, consider a power log-splitter. You can probably get one at the tool rental shop in your town.

• If you have a big, fat stump in your woodpile that looks as if it isn't going to split easily, don't bother trying. That's just the one you need for a chopping block. You've got two? Take the extra in the house for a stool by the fireplace.

• For sawing trees or full-length cordwood into burning lengths, a chainsaw will be fastest. Among the hand-tools, a bowsaw or a bucksaw are best. Cutting firewood with a carpenter's handsaw will wear you out, and chopping it to length with an axe is something you should try

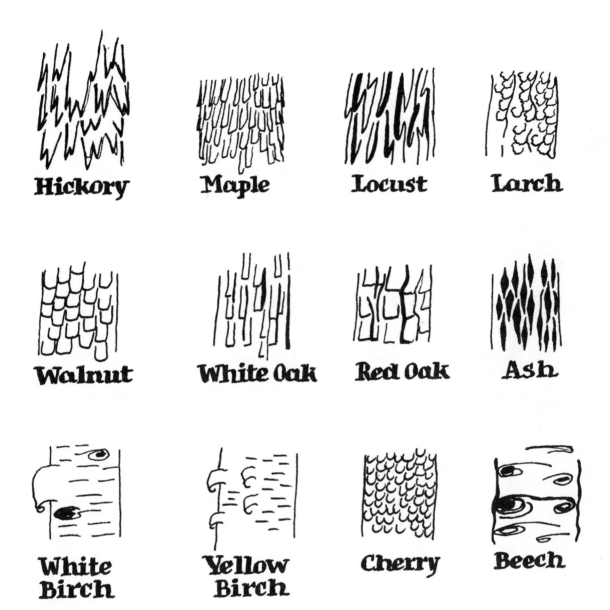

only if your doctor recommends an excess of violent exercise.

• Even the best of us miss a stroke now and then when splitting wood. Don't ignore those chips. Gather them up for starter kindling.

Bow Saw

• Birch logs are pretty just as they are sawn from the tree, but they must be split promptly. Birchbark is almost completely waterproof (the native Americans made canoes from birchbark) and unless you split it, the inside wood will rot quickly and get "punky," rendering it useless for firewood.

All of what has just been said about preparing wood for burning applies to stoves as much as it does to fireplaces, and a good wood stove is many times more fuel-efficient than a fireplace at its best.

The Helpful Wood Stove

Here are some handy wood stove thoughts you can toss in your firebox to see how they burn.

When choosing a wood stove, consider one with a flat top where a pot of water can simmer during the day. It will add needed humidity to your room, and will be ready for cups of tea or coffee without starting up the cooking range.

With a wood stove in your plans, consider a wood-burning cook stove. Some of the models are very attractive, and all have the advantage of saving on kitchen fuel as well as providing room heat.

When starting a stove fire, use rolled paper, slender sticks of kindling, and one or two pieces of split wood. Open all the drafts, get a good fire going, and add more wood when your "starter set" has become a bed of coals. Then adjust the drafts and add more wood as needed when each firing has been reduced to hot coals.

In a well-made, cast-iron wood stove, some sticks just smouldering on a bed of hot coals still put out a lot of good warmth, and they'll quickly spring to a blaze even after several hours as soon as you open the drafts and add a little oxygen from the outside.

A wood stove is most efficient when installed near the center of the house, and on the first floor, or down cellar.

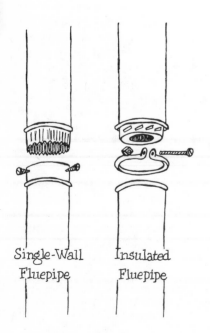

Single-Wall Fluepipe   Insulated Fluepipe

A stove in the cellar will help to keep water pipes from freezing in a winter emergency.

You can always start a stove fire with paper and well-split kindling. If you can't, then check for blockage in your stovepipe draft. Beware of using lighter fluid, gasoline or other such flammables to start an indoor stove fire. You might get more than you bargained for.

You can burn rolled newspapers in your wood stove. One stick of firewood with each two "newspaper logs" makes a good combination, and is a lot better than paying to have the old papers carted away.

BURNING NEWSPAPERS

On my first try with newspaper logs, I soaked a big batch of newspapers in the bathtub, then rolled them tight and tied each "log" with twine. That made a tight roll, but then there was the question of drying them out before burning. I'd made about 150 logs in one batch. They were stacked against the walls all over the house and they represented much more moisture than the rooms wanted. It was many months later before the last of the batch was dry enough to burn. All told, a nuisance.

Now, I just roll them tight by hand right off the old newspaper stack and stuff them in the stove from time to time. Works fine. The coated stock used for printing magazines doesn't burn anywhere near as well.

Coal burns much hotter than wood. If you burn coal in a stove designed for wood, you may overheat the grates and cause them to have a ruinous warp. Yes, you can even open the drafts on a wood fire and get it so hot it will warp the grates and even warp the top of your stove. This is most likely to happen when you're trying to get a wood stove hot too fast. Take it easy. Your stove will get up to best heat in due time. Don't try to force it.

If you are using a woodstove regularly, two woodboxes are a good idea; a larger one for the day's fuel supply, and a smaller one to hold kindling splints. Neither woodbox should touch any part of the stove. That dry wood ignites very easily. Keep it thirty-six inches from the stove.

WHAT THE INSURANCE PEOPLE SAY

Here are the Insurance Underwriter specifications for installing a wood stove.

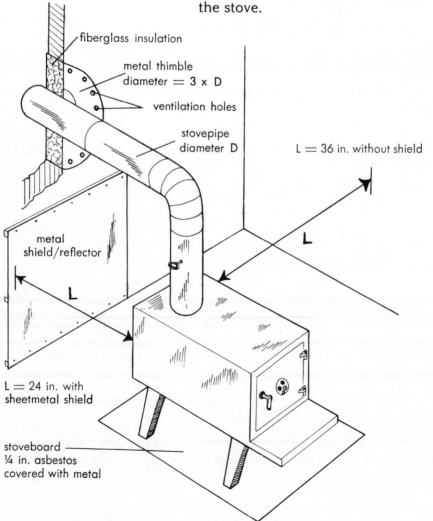

fiberglass insulation

metal thimble diameter = 3 x D

ventilation holes

stovepipe diameter D

L = 36 in. without shield

L

metal shield/reflector

L

L = 24 in. with sheetmetal shield

stoveboard ¼ in. asbestos covered with metal

There's a temptation to use your wood stove as a trash disposer. The best recommendation is—don't. It's an unnecessarily risky way to try to save money. Paper trash and other flash flammables like Christmas tree branches in a fireplace or stove burn too hot, and with big flames that can cause a chimney fire. Artificial logs made of pressed sawdust impregnated with wax, or other artificial compounds can also be dangerous. If a fire gets out of control for any reason, the artificial logs are almost impossible to extinguish.

A brick wall behind your stove will not only make it safer to operate, but will also hold and radiate heat, multiplying your stove's advantages. Careful. Bricks one at a time may not seem to be particularly heavy, but even a modest brick wall can weigh several hundred pounds. Be sure your floor is well enough braced underneath to carry the load of wall plus stove.

When you have a wood stove, give your trash a second look. Anything wood will burn, and broken furniture is almost always good dry hardwood.

Someone taking down a dead tree in the neighborhood may create an opportunity for you when you have a wood stove. Check with the tree crew. Any part of the leftovers they'll put in your yard, or let you haul away, can be either kindling or firewood.

For Safer, Easier Wood-Burning

Here are some ideas that may make your wood-burning easier as well as safer.

• Don't exhaust a wood stove into a flue already in use. Each fire must have a flue of its own.

• Insulated, double-wall stovepipe is your best bet for an outside chimney. There will be less moisture condensation than with single-wall pipe, and therefore less buildup of the flammable carbons and tars that cause chimney fires.

FOR PROTECTION

If you are buying asbestos material for heat insulation for wood stoves, buy asbestos millboard, not asbestos transite (cement) board.

Asbestos transite (cement) board was designed to line boiler rooms and provides little heat resistance. It will conduct heat to any combustible surface to which it is attached. The National Fire Protection Association recommends that asbestos transite board NOT be used as a heat insulator, such as for lining a wall, or for placement under a wood stove.

Asbestos millboard can be used as a heat insulator, both along walls near a wood stove and beneath the stove.

• A heat exchanger for your wood stove fluepipe will in-crease the heat output. There are several designs, all calculated to extract heat from the pipe before the smoke gets outdoors. Some have an electric fan to blow the trapped warmth into the room.

A few final thoughts on heating with wood:

• Maybe your house design will allow a small access hatch between the woodpile and the location of your stove or fireplace. That will eliminate carrying wood in from the outdoors, with resultant opening and closing of doors. A prudent idea.

• A light mist of water sprayed on the ashes in stove or fireplace before you remove them will minimize the "fly ash" spreading around the room. Recycle one of the "spritz" bottles to turn the trick, after it is emptied of its window cleaner, deodorant, or kitchen spray.

Some Old-Timer's Wisdom

9

9

Some Old-Timer's Wisdom

It wasn't so long ago when spun-glass insulation had not been invented, automatic oil burners were still in the future, and triple-track aluminum storm windows hadn't even been thought about. Those days were like today, though, in that people wanted to be comfortable at home in the wintertime.

Lacking many of the innovations of modern technology that we take for granted, they applied their ingenuity to keeping warm and happy while the wind howled around the corners.

We can be no less ingenious in our own time. In fact, there is considerable overlap between yesterday and today. Many of the ideas in this chapter are drawn from the lives of present-day country folk who still practice the arts and idiosyncracies of their forebears. Why? Because the old ways still work.

Some of the ideas may strike you as quaint, corny and impractical. Then there will be the one that strikes you with the ring of reason and you'll try it. And that will be justification enough both for my having written it and your having read it.

There is no intention here to present an exhaustive encyclopedia of pioneer arts. Rather, the intention is to pique your imagination into some new ways of thinking. The ideas here—many of them—are quite individual. The ways in one household were not necessarily the ways in another, because the people were different, and even the houses were different and in their shapes suggested different expedients.

You're different, too, and your house and its living patterns is not exactly like any other on earth. Consider these ideas, then, not only as things you can do, but as guides to a way of thinking. Because we're frugal, we aren't going to supply you with a set of blank pages to continue this exploration on your own, but, in truth, a notebook for jotting down ideas that occur to you isn't a bad idea.

You might also consider some conversation with the oldest members of your family. They'll be pleased that you want to learn from them, and you may hear some great old stories with nuggets of wisdom tucked away in them. The old-timers knew how to have a pretty good life without the advantages and appliances we have. Check it out.

Yesterday's Ideas for Today

Here are some of the old-timers' ideas for keeping warm. If you find you're already using some of them, don't feel you're an old-timer. Instead, look upon yourself as more modern than the rest.

• Consider the humble footstool. Its real purpose was to get your feet up off the floor where the coolest drafts were swirling around. Place a footstool at each comfortable chair in the living room and you might be able to turn down the thermostat by several degrees.

• Keeping your ankles warm contributes greatly to keeping your whole self comfortable. That was the idea behind gaiters, spats, and other ankle-warmers. Try heavy socks for each member of the family to wear in the evening. The kind with leather feet will last longer. Just those warm socks may let you notch down the thermostat a degree or two.

• Another ankle-warmer is tucking a throw rug at the base of each door leading to the outdoors. Even a hardwood doorsill will wear, and then the chills seep through when the wind blows.

• Another way to combat the floor chills is to bank the foundation of the house. Raw dirt used for banking will eventually rot out the wooden sills, but loose straw worked well in the older times, and hay bales are often used today. Another suggestion is to tack or staple builder paper, tar paper or plastic film around the bottom of the house.

• You can often identify an older house by the chimney rising through the middle of the roof. The chimney at the end of the house may have some aesthetic appeal, but most of the warmth it holds will be wasted on the outdoors. That central chimney spread all the warmth it could before the smoke got out.

• At the turn of the century a mark of elegance and luxury was to have high ceilings in the downstairs rooms. It meant you were so wealthy you could afford to heat that extra overhead space. If you have one of those older homes, you might consider installing a drop ceiling, at least down to the tops of the windows. It isn't hard to do, and will save considerably on fuel bills.

• More prudent folks, and those with more modest incomes, often had ceilings as low as seven feet, which is high enough for almost all of us, and makes an easier room to heat. Most modern ceilings are eight feet, principally because standard sheetrock comes in panels eight feet high. You might drop your ceiling down a foot and save on heating bills as well as adding a degree of noise-proofing to the room.

• When you do drop ceilings, all the ceiling electrical fixtures must be changed. Consider putting translucent panels in your drop ceiling grid, with simple fluorescent lights above them. The fluorescents are less expensive to operate and will give the room a friendly glow.

THE BEST BOOKCASES

My maternal grandfather was a scholar and teacher, so naturally he had a lot of books. His bookcases had sliding glass doors, which offered a double advantage. With the doors closed his books didn't get dusty—and dusting books is a miserable chore. The second advantage was that with the doors closed the bookcases were closed space that didn't need to be heated.

• Maybe you don't need ceiling lights at all. Lighting the individual places where people are reading or working will be less expensive than lighting a whole room.

• In former times, folks carried their lights with them as they traveled from room to room in the evening, instead of having the whole house lighted. The traveling light was most often a candle in a holder with a handle, or perhaps an oil lamp.

• When your back is warm, you're likely to feel warmer all over. That's probably why the vest and the sleeveless sweater were invented. If you buy or make one of these, be sure it's long enough in back to keep you covered when you bend over or lift your arms.

• Another traditional body-warmer is the friendly afghan. Originally this was a small rug from Afghanistan, and later the term came to be applied to many different designs of small blankets knitted or crocheted at home.

Each well-equipped home had at least one afghan, draped over the end of the couch in the living room. It wasn't just a decoration. It was used for keeping the legs warm.

• You may have noticed that many of the old four-poster beds were perched on long, sturdy legs rather high off the floor. Well, the closer you get to the ceiling, the warmer it is. There was a practical purpose in that design.

• Three or four blankets get terribly heavy during the night. One alternative is the electric blanket, but it keeps the meter running. The old-timers counted on the down-filled comforter to keep them warm. It's a winner.

• The coverlet or bedspread on George Washington's bed was probably more than just a decorative item or a dust-cover. It was likely a closely-woven, hand-loomed cover made of linsey-woolsey—a mixture of linen and wool. It's a warm combination, particularly when paired with that down comforter.

• You've heard jokes about the Saturday night bath. It wasn't a joke at the turn of the century. Water was heated in pots on the kitchen range and poured into the big family washtub. The little ones bathed first, then the adults. It may not have been the most sanitary of customs, but really, how unsanitary are little tads going to get?

• Another old-time favorite was the bed-warmer—a covered, shallow brass pan with a long handle. Hot coals from the fire were put in the pan, then it was passed between the sheets just before bedtime. Delightful. The brass bed-warmer also worked for roasting chestnuts, and later generations have used it for making popcorn.

• Many of the older homes have a piece of furniture you might not be able to identify. It's a combination mitten-warmer and towel rack. Small enough to be moved easily

BED-WARMERS

We lived out past the end of the power lines for awhile when I was young, so winter warmth was achieved old-style. Each of us kids had a good-sized round stone as a personal possession. (You could use a brick.) Each night our stones were heated in the oven of the kitchen range, then my mother would wrap each one in soft flannel and put it in the foot of the bed. Nothing quite like that warm, flannel-wrapped stone to greet your toes as you push down through the cool sheets.

to just the right distance from the stove, it would dry out soggy mittens, have warm towels ready for the bath (what a luxury!), and even line up the boots to dry. It was made from pine planks and discarded broomstick handles—not a fancy item, but a nifty. You could make one, and it would be worth its small effort if for nothing more than those warm towels.

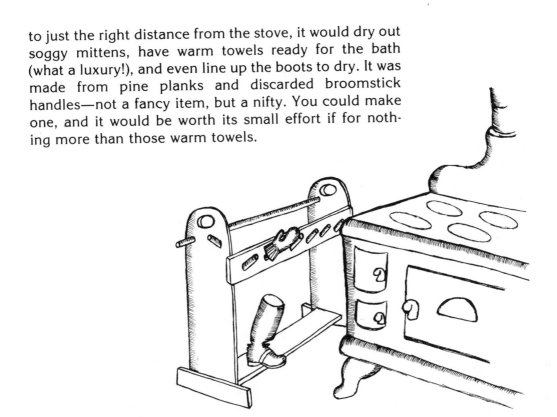

• Today, almost all the shutters you see are purely decorative. Yesterday, they were part of the heating and cooling system. They would be closed on cold winter nights, and those on the sunny side would be closed to keep out sun heat on hot summer days.

• That big country kitchen was a homey place. In the winter, it was also the warmest place in the house, so it made sense that the kitchen was big enough for the whole family. With a lamp on the kitchen table, everyone would gather around the light in the warm room to finish homework, read, play games, or just munch on fresh cookies and chat.

• Many of the older homes had a summer kitchen added to the back of the house. It had a stove, a sink, and some storage space so cooking could be carried on without

heating up the main house. The sink had a drain, but no running water, so there were no pipes to freeze in the winter. Off season, the summer kitchen was used as an unheated storage room.

HOMEMADE ICE CREAM

The most eagerly anticipated summertime treat at our house when I was young was home-made ice cream. It was worth the effort of cranking the dasher for the delicious result. There are now electric ice-cream makers, and mixes that will make a cold something in the freezer compartment of your refrigerator, but nothing will match the product of that old hand-cranked model. Try it with fresh peaches or fresh strawberries in the mix. Super!

• Many of the old wood-fired kitchen ranges had a warming oven at eye-level. The flue-pipe passed through it to give it a moderate temperature. Breads, muffins, rolls, and pies were popped in the warming oven for a little time before serving, and often the dinner plates were warmed there, too—a custom now practiced in the finest and most expensive restaurants.

• A cousin to the man's necktie and the woman's fashionable scarf—both relatively useless items of apparel—is that snuggly old item, the shawl. Girls knitted them for their beaux; grandmothers crocheted them for grandchildren; almost everybody wore them, both indoors and out. They were a most handy way to put on a little extra warmth around the neck and shoulders: less cumbersome than a jacket, less likely to muss the hair than a sweater. They were often made of light wool yarns in neutral colors such as grey, tan, and light blue that would harmonize with almost anything. A favorite shawl was a lifetime treasure. Usually wider and lighter in weight than what we would call a scarf, the shawl deserves a revival.

Taming the Guzzler

10

Taming the Guzzler

If there is one reality that immediately identifies American society it is the automobile. Not only has the horse and buggy disappeared, but the passenger railroad train has almost followed the trolley car down the tracks to nowhere. We're hooked on personal transportation in the form of that wonder of the modern world, the private motorcar.

And we love it. Even the most environmentally concerned go to meetings in cars, so there will be no suggestions here about abandoning the automobile. It's accepted as a central fact for more years to come than this book will be in print.

The question is: How do you live with it and not go broke?

If you're this far along it's assumed you have a car or two, so you already know about the upward spiral in the cost of petroleum products. You've considered, or are already driving, a compact or sub-compact to economize at the gas pump, but it seems that every prudent step you take is canceled by the Seven Sisters (which is inside talk for the seven major international oil companies).

Are we doomed to rolling poverty? Not necessarily.

There are some basic principles that can be stated.

Your car isn't only toting you from here to there, it's toting itself. The less weight the engine must haul around, the more efficiently it will perform. Therefore, the smaller and lighter the car you can comfortably drive, the less it will cost to operate. The auto manufacturers have gotten this message, so there are plenty of choices among the lighter weight cars.

The fewer the horses you have to feed to get you from here to there, the less it will cost. The big twelve- and sixteen-cylinder yachts-on-wheels that were the luxury cars of a generation ago aren't even available today unless you have one custom built, in which case you probably aren't reading this book. They revved up a lot of horsepower that wasn't needed.

Check Your Driving Habits

Your driving habits are a key to economical operation of your car. The place to begin understanding those habits is with a miles-per-gallon record that will take the guesswork out of driving economy.

The first place to apply that mpg record is in the regular trips you make, as in driving to work. You may be following a traffic flow, or going by what you think is the shortest way, but that may not be the cheapest route. If there are alternative ways from home to job, or any other regular destination, take the trouble to check them out for mileage efficiency. You may wind up going a new way.

The reason an alternative route may be less costly is that your car operates most efficiently at a steady speed. If the shorter route has lots of stops and starts it probably

will burn more gas than a longer way around that lets you keep an even pace.

The other way to get there may have fewer stoplights. Good. With your engine idling you'll burn a gallon of gas in fifty minutes, going nowhere. Lots of zero-miles-per-gallon waiting at stoplights and stop signs can be expensive over the course of a year. Have the right change ready at toll booths on your way for minimum waiting time.

The most economical driving in any car is when you are just feeding enough gas to maintain momentum at a steady speed on the level. Build up that momentum in as relaxed a way as you can, consistent with the traffic flow. That means easy starts away from your driveway, away from the traffic lights—every time you are accelerating.

Remember, every time you touch the brakes you are paying to reduce the momentum that cost so much to build up. Watch the traffic signs and ease off gradually instead of having to use your brakes to get to a slower speed.

Tailgating—driving too close to the guy in front—puts your driving pace at the mercy of his whims. As a tailgater you'll be alternately braking and pumping gas as you respond to the forward driver's perception of the road, which is different from yours. Tailgating is not only hazardous, it's expensive.

A quick jab at the gas pedal, or pumping the pedal, squirts raw gas into the engine's combustion system. Trying to get started, you can flood your engine that

A CHEAP START

We have a downhill driveway, followed by a downhill stretch of road before we hit much traffic. With the standard transmission car we have, there are times in the winter when we start rolling, rather than cranking the engine and pumping gas to get started. Easy. Cheap.

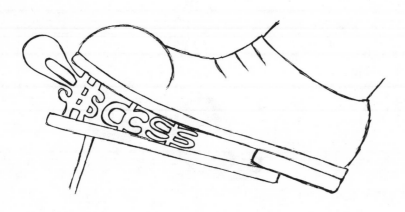

way, as you have probably already discovered. A smooth, steady pressure on the gas pedal is always a money-saver.

When you're approaching an uphill climb, there's a money-saving technique to use. Build up a little extra momentum as you approach the base, then keep it steady or even ease off a little as you are climbing. Trying to add speed as you are climbing a hill is one of the most expensive maneuvers you can devise. If you're driving a low-horsepower car uphill, be prepared to downshift rather than feed more gas in high gear. It's cheaper.

If you have a choice when you are traveling, make your stops on a downhill slope. Starting from scratch is much cheaper when you're rolling downhill.

Resist the temptation to coast on a long downhill. In many states this practice is illegal, and for good reasons: it's dangerous. When coasting, you don't have the control of your car that is possible with the engine engaged. Your brakes can overheat and fade away; you run the hazard of locking your steering wheel in some cars, and you'll save very little gas. When going downhill leave the engine engaged, but take your foot off the gas, or touch the pedal oh-so-lightly.

Ease off on the speed. A car that gets forty miles-per-gallon at forty miles an hour might get as little as twenty-five miles-per-gallon at seventy. A ten-mile trip flat-out at sixty will take ten minutes. It will only take two minutes longer at fifty, and that kind of difference can be blown away at a stoplight, or looking for a place to park.

Either with air conditioning in the summer, or with the heater in the winter, the natural flow of air makes using the blower fan unnecessary at over forty miles per hour. Since the fan itself can subtract as much as 1 mile-per-gallon to operate, that's something to consider, particularly on a long trip.

In the winter, start off slowly in a cold car. All the lubricants are like molasses for a mile or two. They'll loosen up, and then your engine won't need to work so hard to keep you moving at highway speed. A short warm-up of the engine before starting can also help

MAKE A LIST

We live about twenty-five miles from town, so we make lists before we go shopping.

It's a pain in the neck to get back home and discover we've forgotten something. The household shopping list is an excellent idea. It not only cuts down the number of shopping trips, but also makes each trip one that can be planned for minimum mileage.

We find that the combination trip is useful. Going to church in town is combined with a visit with some friends and relations; a scheduled trip to the dentist is put together with shopping, buying postage stamps, and getting the dog to the vet. Some household cooperation gets more accomplished with minimum mileage.

reduce engine wear, since the first ten minutes are the hardest-wearing—especially in cold weather.

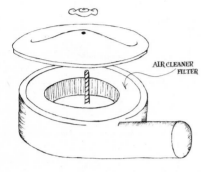

AIR CLEANER FILTER

CHECK YOUR TIRES

Let's take a look at the tires.

Your owner's manual has important information on your tires, including the air pressure that should be in them. Underinflation of your tires can cost you as much as one mile per gallon; overinflation will wear the tires out sooner. You can buy a small pressure gauge and check the pressure yourself from time to time more accurately than the reading on the gas station air-pump.

Radial tires have 50 percent less road resistance, and so they give you from 3 to 10 percent better miles per gallon. They also wear about three times as long, so they're a good buy even though they are expensive.

Radial snow tires also have less road resistance than conventional winter shoes, while still giving necessary road traction.

How to Stretch a Tank of Gas

You can get 6 to 20 percent better mpg with a properly tuned engine. Keeping a mileage record will tell you when your mpg is slipping, which is a signal for a tune-up.

There are a few items you can take care of easily without going to a garage. One of them is the air filter. A clogged air filter leaves your engine gasping for breath and means you're probably running with a "rich" mixture, that is, more gas and less air. Many chain and auto stores carry air filters and they are simple to change. A clogged air filter can cost you 1 mpg. Fix it.

Dirty oil cuts back engine efficiency. You can change your own, and buying your own oil is much cheaper than getting it at a gas station. There's a drain plug under your engine that will come out readily with a wrench. Have a bucket ready to catch the dirty oil.

If your fan belt is too tight, your engine is working too hard and wasting gas. The belt should give a little to finger pressure when the engine is not running. If it doesn't, the adjustment is easy to make with a wrench.

Badly worn spark plugs can cost you as much as 2 mpg. You'll need a special wrench to remove the spark plugs for inspection, and when you get them out you may not know a good one from a bad one. This is probably a job for a trained technician. If you decide to check the plugs yourself, be sure you mark the leads to the distributor cap before taking them off the plugs, so you can get them back on in the proper order.

The plugs may need just a little elementary cleaning you can do by scraping with a jacknife blade. If one of the plugs looks very different from the others—it's very oily, or blacker, or badly pitted—you have a situation that calls for a trained mechanic.

11

Your Next House

The average American family moves from one home to another every five years. Considering that group of folks who settle down and stay as a part of that average, most of us move fairly often.

With that thought in mind, it seemed worthwhile to consider some of the factors you might have in mind when you're looking for your next house. Maybe you'll be building from scratch; maybe you'll be shopping for a house someone else built, but either way you can look for advantages that wouldn't be practical to build into your present home.

Little can be done to minimize the disadvantages of the rambling ranch, and trying to insulate an older home can be an expensive and discouraging proposition. You can keep those realities in mind as you shop.

You'll probably get closest to the ideal if you're in a position to build from the ground up, so much of this chapter makes that assumption. Even if that's not your situation, you can be looking for the home you would build if you could.

Often, successful living is the art of compromise. You'll be weighing one set of criteria against another set, and deciding where the compromises must be made. One can hope that with the ideas here the continuing cost factors will be weighed in the balance, so you'll have some money left after the monthly bills are paid.

And, when looking for a new home, you can be making mental assessments as to the feasibility of modifications and adaptations that will make daily living more practical. Moving the structure to another position on the land may be impossible. Insulating the garage area so it doesn't borrow home heat is easy and inexpensive in many situations.

Let's assume our search is in an area where the seasons include real winter months. Here we go.

Study the Home's Setting

If you're looking at home sites in a hilly area, the best location is on a southeast slope. A little rise to the west will tend to cut the force of the prevailing winds in winter, and the southern exposure will both take maximum advantage of the southern sun for winter heating, and give the best prospects for gardening in the summer.

Having picked an ideal location, you will be best off if the principal windows face south, and the structure is positioned on an east-west axis to provide a south-facing roof. Deep overhanging eaves on the south side will let you take maximum advantage of the winter sunlight, while shading you from the direct heat of the summer sun.

Broad-leafed trees on the south side of your house will make a cooling shade in the summer, then conveniently drop their leaves and let the winter sun warmth through, just when you want it.

A solid windbreak of hardy evergreens to the west of your house, and some more on the north side, will be a welcome shield from winter winds, and will break the sunbeams in the heat of the late afternoon in summer.

A light-colored roof will reflect heat; a dark-colored roof will absorb heat. With a truss roof and just waste space above the ceiling, that roof color factor won't make a lot of difference. If there is usable space under the roof and adequate ventilation available, the dark-roof option will save money during the winter months.

Small windows on the north side will provide summer cross-ventilation and minimum exposure to winter cold. Be sure those north windows are double-glazed, or

BONANZA

I had a chance one time to buy an old, run-down farmhouse. The place needed a lot of work, but I was glad to do it because on the property were apple, cherry, plum, peach, and quince trees, grape vines, and several kinds of berry bushes. A bonanza! Where I live now didn't even have functional plumbing when I moved in, but it did have apple and cherry trees, raspberry, blackberry and currant bushes, and a fine stand of sugar maples. Worth looking for.

A LUCKY BREAK

For some reason the remodeled schoolhouse where I live had its west-facing windows boarded over many years ago. When I added a wing, it was positioned on the west side and the design called for no windows in the west end of the wing. It would be nice if I could take credit for brilliant planning, but I didn't know how smart I was. If you can arrange it, no windows in the west wall facing the prevailing winds is a good idea. I got lucky.

covered with storm windows. It may even be prudent to put storm windows over double-glazed windows on the north side.

A big front yard is just a place to spend time with a lawnmower, and it assures a long driveway to plow after every snowstorm. Look for the bigger space out back where it can be put to good use as a vegetable garden.

A Close Look At the House

If the grounds satisfy you, it's time to study the house itself—closely.

The two-story design is far more economical than the extended single-floor plan. The principal heat loss in a house is through the roof, so the less roof you have, the less it will cost to heat.

If you are building your own home, consider using 2x6's instead of the usual 2x4's in framing outside walls. This will permit the use of a heavier layer of insulation. A bonus advantage is an interesting window option; you can set your windows flush with the outer wall and give yourself deep windowsills indoors, or you can do the opposite for an unusual deep-set window effect from the outside.

A house that is planned for energy saving will have an unheated garage, woodshed, or toolshed shielding a west or north wall. The buffer space of those unheated rooms is excellent insulation.

Many contemporary designs locate closets and other storage spaces in the house interior, because they don't need the windows that are associated with outer walls. The center of the house, though, will be the warmest place in winter, and not the most sensible place for storage. Try for a design that puts closets and storage spaces on north and west outer walls, where they can serve as insulators.

Functions that require plumbing will be clustered, that is, the kitchen, bath, and laundry will be as close to each other as possible. This is easier in a two-story design.

YEAR-ROUND COMFORT

The wing we built on the schoolhouse is half below grade and we located three bedrooms there. Their windows are smaller and higher up the wall than they might otherwise be, but since bedrooms are used primarily at night, the size and placement of windows isn't critical. The downstairs bedrooms are easy to heat in winter, and stay cool for summer sleeping.

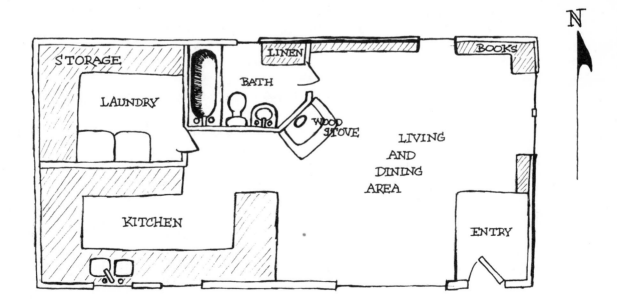

That way the water and drain lines will be short (which will save money for openers if you're doing the installing), making them easier to secure in a wintertime heating emergency. Also, short hot water lines keep the water warmer between heater and faucet.

Rooms that may be unused in winter should not have water lines running through them. Given the absence of water lines, and separate room thermostats, the extra rooms can be shut off when they are not in use. There's a money-saver.

Separate thermostats, or adjustable registers, for each room in the house will give you the kind of control of room warmth you need, to recapture control of your total heating budget.

Consider getting along without general, full-room illumination for evenings. The wall switches at the room entry can be wired to plug outlets where individual lamps can be positioned.

Where full-room illumination is indicated, as, perhaps, kitchen or playroom, get acquainted with the varieties of fluorescent fixtures. The cool tubes use just one-fifth the power of incandescent light bulbs, and are available in warm color tones that are much easier on the eyes than the original mortuary blue.

When buying or building, give a thought to chimney placement. The central chimney will radiate warmth whenever the heating unit is in use. If you are planning to use one or more wood stoves, be sure your house design allows for easy chimney placement.

When building your own home, consider ceilings as low as seven feet six inches, or even seven feet. You'll trim a chunk off your heating bill, and the height will accommodate all but a handful of professional basketball players.

A final consideration:

You may not want to build or buy a solar home now, but will the design of the house you are thinking about adapt to solar installation at a later date? It's called retrofitting. If the principal roof area is facing south, you're on the way to a solar water heater, and then complete solar heat.